DUBLIN
Baile átha
COLOUR STREET ATLAS & GUIDE

GEOGRAPHIA

The greatest care and attention is taken when we produce these atlases but, if you find any errors, we would be grateful to hear from you.

If you wish to send us information relating to this product, please contact:-

The Chief Cartographer,
Geographia Limited,
105 / 107 Bath Road,
Cheltenham,
Glos. GL53 7LE

© Geographia 1990
Geographia is an imprint of Bartholomew - the Cartographic Division of the Collins Publishing Group

Based on the Ordnance Survey by permission of the Government of the Republic of Ireland
(Permit number 4454)

First Edition 1988
Reprinted 1990

Information Section © Geographia Ltd, 1988

Great care has been taken throughout this book to be accurate but the publishers cannot accept responsibility for any errors which appear, or their consequences.

Printed in Scotland by John Bartholomew & Son Ltd.

Contents - Legend

Contents

Page 4-7 Ireland Route Planner

8-17 Dublin City Guide

Including:
History • Tourist Information Offices • Cathedrals • Churches • Museums • Interesting Buildings and Places • Libraries • Galleries • Theatres • Cinemas • Public Houses • Restaurants • Passenger Travel • Hotels • Shops • Markets • Social and Welfare • Hospitals • Embassies • Sports Venues and Clubs • Car Repairs

18-19 Key to City Maps

20-63 City Maps

64-79 Index to Street Names

Legend

——■—— Railways and Railway Stations

2 Postal Boundaries

—·—·— City Boundaries

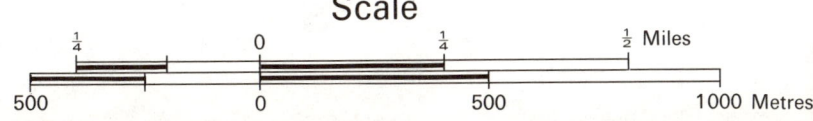

Ireland Route Planner

Ireland Route Planner

Dublin City Guide

HISTORY

The ford over the River Liffey has been important since Celtic times, and there was a thriving Christian community here from the 5thC, following their conversion by St Patrick in AD448. In AD840 the marauding Vikings landed here, built a fortress on the high ground and established a settlement along the banks of the estuary. Originally a base for their numerous raiding sorties, it soon became a flourishing trading port as well, but Viking dominance was severely curtailed following a defeat by Brian Boru at the Battle of Clontarf in 1014.

Converted to Christianity, the Vikings were finally driven out by the Anglo-Normans under Strongbow, who took Dublin by storm, executing the Viking leader, Hasculf. In 1172 Henry II, having established his feudal rights over the invading force, received the submission of the Irish chieftains on the site of College Green. He granted the city by charter to the men of Bristol, from whence the Anglo-Normans had originally come.

The city and surrounding area, established as the seat of English government and protected by an enclosing wall and strategic castles, was known as The Pale. Frequently attacked during the 12thC and 13thC by the Irish clans based in the Wicklow Mountains, it was assaulted unsuccessfully by Edward Bruce in 1316. The city witnessed the crowning of Lambert Simnel, pretender to the English throne, in Christ Church in 1486. Unmoved by the rebellion of 'Silken' Thomas Fitzgerald in 1534, the inhabitants remained loyal to the English crown, supporting King Charles during the Civil Wars. Captured by the Parliamentarians in 1647, the city underwent a great architectural expansion following the Restoration of Charles II. During the Williamite wars Dublin was a Jacobite stronghold. It was here that James II held his last parliament in 1689.

By the end of the 17thC, Dublin was already a flourishing commercial centre; public street lighting had been introduced in 1697 and during the following century the city was transformed into one of the handsomest of Georgian cities. The 'Wide Streets Commission' was established in 1757 and in 1773 the Paving Board was formed. New, elegantly spacious streets and squares were planned and palatial town houses built. In 1783 the Irish Parliament was granted a short-lived autonomy but there was growing political unrest, which erupted in the uprising of 1798. Lord Edward Fitzgerald died of wounds sustained resisting arrest and in 1800 the detested Act of Union was established and the fortunes of the city began to wane.

With government now in London, few of the noblemen required their fine mansions and many returned to their country estates or left for London. Bitterness increased; in 1803 the Lord Chief Justice was assassinated and Robert Emmet, the leader of an abortive insurrection, was hanged. The newspaper *The Nation* was established by Charles Gavan Duffy in 1842, the heyday of the Repeal Movement. In 1841 Daniel O'Connell was elected Lord Mayor; only three years later he was interned in Richmond Gaol for campaigning for the repeal of the Union and the restoration of Grattan's 'Irish Parliament'. In 1873 the first great Home Rule Conference was held. In 1879 the Land League was formed, whose leaders, including Parnell and Davitt, were imprisoned for their pains. In 1882 the new Chief Secretary, Lord Frederick Cavendish, and his Under-Secretary were assassinated in Phoenix Park by the Invincibles, a new terrorist organisation. As the campaign for Home Rule gathered momentum, the Gaelic League, which started the Irish literary renaissance, was established by Douglas Hyde and Eóin MacNeill in 1893. Conceived as a means of reviving interest in the Irish language and traditional Irish life, the Gaelic League was also responsible for a remarkable literary revival resulting in the formation of the Abbey Theatre in 1904, where plays by J M Synge, Sean O'Casey and W B Yeats, amongst others, were performed.

In 1905 the Sinn Fein movement was formed, in 1909 the Irish Transport and General Workers Union was set up under the leadership of James Connolly, and in 1913 there was a massive strike, paralysing the city. In 1914 the Irish Volunteers came into being, largely to combat the Ulster Volunteers. These latter were raised by Edward Carson in January 1913 to defend the right of Ulster to remain united with Great Britain. In 1916 the Irish Volunteers seized the Post Office in Lower O'Connell Street as their

Dublin City Guide

headquarters and the Easter Rising had begun. It was quickly crushed, but so brutally that public conscience, clearly appalled, overwhelmingly elected Sinn Fein at the general election of December 1918 with de Valera as the new president. Whilst the Dublin faction were openly in support of the guerrilla bands operating across the country, the Ulster Unionists set up their own provisional government, and the ambushes and assassinations which characterised the Anglo-Irish War, featuring the notorious Black and Tans, began in bloody earnest. The war ended in the truce of July 1921. Despite the ratification of the Irish Free State in January 1922, a large and dissatisfied faction of leaders in the Irish movement took up arms against their former comrades and seized the Four Courts, which they held for two months. The subsequent shelling ordered by the new Dublin Government destroyed much of O'Connell Street but by the 1930s most of the public buildings had been restored.

TOURIST INFORMATION OFFICES

Dublin City 14 Upper O'Connell Street, Dublin 1. Tel: (01) 747733. Telex: 32462.

Dublin Airport Tel: (01) 376387/(01) 375533. Telex: 32491.

CATHEDRALS AND CHURCHES

Christchurch Cathedral Christchurch Place.
The Cathedral was founded by Strongbow in 1173 on the site of a church founded in 1038 by Dunan, Bishop of Dublin. It is, along with St Patrick's, one of the best examples in Ireland of early Gothic architecture, and was extensively restored between 1871–78 by George Edmund Street.

Christ Church Cathedral (CI)

St Patrick's Cathedral Patrick Street.
The National Cathedral of the Church of Ireland, it was built between 1220–54 and was restored in the 19thC.
St Audoen's Church High Street.
Dublin's only surviving medieval church, with a portal of 1190. The bell tower, restored in the 19thC., has three 15thC. bells.

St. Audoen's Church (CI)

St Werburgh's Church Werburgh Street.
Originally the site of an Anglo-Norman foundation, the present church was built in 1715–19 and rebuilt in 1759–68, following a fire.
St Michan's Church Church Street.
Founded in 1095 and largely rebuilt in 1685. Famous for the mummified bodies in the crypt and its fine 18thC. organ.
St Audoen's RC Church High Street.
Designed by Patrick Byrne in 1841–47, it has a monumental, cliff-like exterior with a huge Corinthian portico added by Stephen Ashlin in 1898.
St Mary's Abbey Meetinghouse Lane.
A Cistercian foundation, established in 1139, whose remains include a fine vaulted Chapter House of 1190.
Augustinian Church Thomas Street.
Designed by E W Pugin and G C Ashlin in 1862 it has a mountainous exterior with lofty side aisles to the nave and 160-foot-high tower crowned by a spire.

Dublin City Guide

St Saviour's Dominick Street.
Designed by J J McCarthy in 1858 this extravagant French-style Gothic edifice has a bold west door under a triangular hood, crowned by a large rose window.
St Stephen's Mount Street Crescent.
Designed by John Bowden in 1824 this handsome neo-classical church has a Erechtheon-inspired Greek-style portico.
St Mary's Pro-Cathedral Cathedral Street.
A Greek Doric-style building, built 1815–25 by John Sweetman and modelled on the Church of St Philippe, Rue St Honore, Paris.
St Mary's Mary Street.
A handsome galleried church designed by Thomas Burgh in 1627.
St George's Temple Street.
This neo-classical church was designed by Francis Johnston in 1802 and has a 200-foot-high steeple modelled on St Martin-in-the-Fields, London.
Franciscan Church Merchant's Quay.
Designed by Patrick Byrne in 1830.
St Anne's Church Dawson Street.
Designed by Isaac Wells in 1720 with a Romanesque-style facade added by Sir Thomas Deane in 1868.

INTERESTING BUILDINGS

General Post Office O'Connell Street.
Designed by Francis Johnston and completed in 1818. The 1916 Easter Rising started here.
Custom House Custom House Quay.
This masterpiece was designed by James Gandon in 1781 and although not open to the public, has a magnificent long river frontage.
Dublin Castle Cork Hill, Dame Street.
The Castle was originally built 1204–28 as part of Dublin's defensive system. The Record or Wardrobe Tower is the principal remnant of the 13thC. Anglo-Norman fortress and has walls 16 foot thick.

The 15thC Bermingham Tower was once the state prison where Red Hugh O'Donnell was interned in the 16thC. Of interest are the State Apartments, dating from the British Administration; these were once the residence of English Viceroys.
Trinity College College Green.
The original Elizabethan college was founded in 1592 but the present building was built between 1755–1759. The cruciform complex wrapped around quadrangles and gardens has an impressive 300-foot Palladian facade designed by Henry Keene and John Sanderford.

The library's great treasures include the 8thC. Book of Kells, the Book of Durrow, the Book of Armagh and the Liber Hymnorum.
Leinster House Kildare Street.
Originally a handsome town mansion designed by Richard Castle for the Earl of Kildare in 1745; it has been the Parliament House since 1922.
Bank of Ireland College Green.
Designed by Sir Edward Lovett Pearce in 1729. It was originally the Parliament House; the first of a series of great public buildings erected in 18thC. Dublin.
Four Courts Inns Quay.
Originally designed by James Gandon in 1785, it was destroyed by a fire in 1922 but later rebuilt. Four Courts has a 450-foot river frontage and a square central block with circular hall, crowned by a shallow dome carried in a high-columned drum.
Guinness Brewery St James Gate.
Established in 1759 and is now the largest exporting brewery in the world. The Guinness Hop Store is open to the public Mon–Fri 10 am to 3 pm. Tel: 536700.
Kilmainham Jail Inchicore.
Built in 1796. Countless patriots have been imprisoned here including Emmet and his United Irishmen colleagues, the Fenians, the Invincibles and the Irish Volunteers of the Easter Rising. It was closed in 1924 and re-opened as a museum in 1966.
Malahide Castle Malahide.
Originally built in 1185, it was the seat of the Talbot family from 1185–1976. Now in public ownership, it displays a large part of the National Portrait collection.
Marino Casino Malahide Road.
A miniature Palladian-style masterpiece designed by Sir William Chambers in 1762. Built as a little pleasure house beside Lord Charlemont's country residence for the enormous sum of £60,000, it's a remarkably compact building planned in a Greek cross articulated by both free-standing columns and pilasters with rusticated main walls. The circular hall inside, ringed by columns, is crowned by a coffered dome. The graceful urns crowning the attic storey are chimneys.

Dublin City Guide

Mansion House Dawson Street.
Built in 1705, it has been the official residence of the Lord Mayor of Dublin since 1715.

Mansion House

Powerscourt House South William Street.
A classical-style mansion designed by Robert Mack and built 1771–74.

PLACES OF INTEREST

Wood Quay by Christchurch Cathedral.
Modern office blocks and new civic offices occupy this site which was once the 9th–11thC Viking city of Dublin.
Garden of Remembrance Parnell Square.
The Garden of Remembrance, opened in 1966, dedicated to all those who died in the cause of Irish Freedom.
Arbour Hill Collins Barracks.
Cemetery where the leaders of the Easter Rising are buried.
Dunsink Observatory between Finglas and Blanchardstown.
Founded in 1783, it is one of the oldest observatories in the world. Public nights are held on the first and third Saturdays of each month from September to March inclusive at 8 pm–10 pm.

MUSEUMS

National Museum Kildare Street. Tel: 765521.
Houses a fabulous collection of national antiquities including Bronze Age gold ornaments.
Dublin Civic Museum South William Street. Tel: 794260.
Permanent exhibition about the city of Dublin.
Museum of Childhood Palmerston Park, Rathmines. Tel: 973223.
Charming private collection of antique dolls and toys.
National Wax Museum Parnell Square. Tel: 746416.
Wax replicas of well-known persons and scenes.
Museum of Broadcasting Lower Rathmines Road. Tel: 905798.
Illustrates the progress of Irish radio and TV over the last 60 years.
Pearse Museum St. Enda's Park, Rathfarnham. Tel: 934208.
Dedicated to Patrick Pearse, the leader of the Easter Rising, and his family.
Garda Siochana Museum Phoenix Park. Tel: 771156.
Display of materials, uniforms, equipment, photographs and medals depicting the history of the Irish Police.
James Joyce Museum Sandycove. Tel: 809265.
Personal possessions, photographs, first editions and items about James Joyce.
Kilmainham Jail Inchicore Road. Tel: 535990.
Museum dedicated to the Irish patriots imprisoned there from 1792–1924.
Natural History Museum Leinster Lawn.
Houses a collection of preserved animals and the remains of extinct mammals and birds.
Guinness Hop Store St James Gate. Tel: 536700.
Documentary films and exhibition about the company's development.
Irish Architectural Archive Merrion Square. Tel: 763430.
National Maritime Museum Haigh Terrace, Dun Laoghaire. Tel: 800969.
Aeronautical Museum Dublin Airport. Tel: 376387.

Dublin City Guide

LIBRARIES

National Library Kildare Street.
Tel: 765521.
Offers over half a million books, as well as a vast collection of maps, prints and manuscripts and an invaluable collection of Irish newspapers.
Trinity College Library College Green.
Tel: 772941.
The oldest and most famous of Dublin's libraries; it houses over a million books plus a magnificent collection of early illuminated manuscripts, including the famous Book of Kells.
Royal Irish Academy Dawson Street.
Tel: 762570.
One of the largest collections of ancient Irish manuscripts in the country.
Pearse Street Library Pearse Street.
Tel: 777662.
Irish interest books including references to local printing and bookbinding.
Marsh's Library St Patrick's Close.
Tel: 753917.
Opened in 1701, contains many rare books.
Kings Inns Henrietta Street.
Tel: 747134.
Founded 1787, contains over 100,000 books and copies of almost all of the Dublin directories ever published.
Central Catholic Library Merrion Square.
Tel: 761264.
Religious and general interest, with a large Irish section.
Goethe Institute Library Merrion Square.
Tel: 611155.
A business information centre.
Chester Beatty Library & Gallery of Oriental Art Shrewsbury Road.
Tel: 692386.
Houses one of the finest collections of oriental manuscripts and miniatures in the world.

Other general and reference libraries:
Dublin Diocesan Library Clonliffe Road.
Tel: 741680.
Genealogical Office Adelaide Road.
Tel: 614877.
Central Library Ilac Centre. Tel: 734333.
Music Lending Library, Community, Youth and Information Library.
Gilbert Library Pearse Street.
Tel: 777662.

GALLERIES, ARTS CENTRES, CONCERT AND EXHIBITION HALLS

Alliance Francaise Kildare Street.
Tel: 761732.
Ballsbridge Gallery Baggot Lane.
Tel: 600363.
City Centre Art Centre Tel: 770643.
Cynthia O'Connor Gallery Kildare Street.
Tel: 792177.
Davis Gallery Capel Street.
Tel: 726969.
Douglas Hyde Gallery Trinity College.
Tel: 772941 Ext 1116.
Gallery of Photography Wellington Quay.
Tel: 714654.
Grace Pym Gallery Duke Street.
Tel: 770416.
Grafton Gallery St Annes Lane.
Tel: 791835.
Hendriks Gallery St Stephens Green.
Tel: 756062.
Lincoln Gallery Lincoln Place.
Tel: 680665.
Municipal Gallery Parnell Square.
Tel: 741903.
National Gallery Merrion Square.
Tel: 615133.
Neptune Gallery South William Street.
Tel: 715021.
Oliver Dowling Kildare Street.
Tel: 766573.
Oriel Gallery Clare Street.
Tel: 763410.
Patrick Brown Gallery South William Street. Tel: 719013.
Project Arts Centre East Essex.
Tel: 712321.
Solomon Gallery Powerscourt Centre.
Tel: 794237.
Taylor Gallery Dawson Street.
Tel: 776089.
Tom Caldwell Gallery Upper Fitzwilliam Street. Tel: 688629.
United Arts Club Upper Fitzwilliam Street. Tel: 762965.
Bank of Ireland Exhibition Hall Lower Baggot Street. Tel: 785744.
Royal Dublin Society Ballsbridge.
Tel: 680645.
National Concert Hall Earlsfort Terrace.
Tel: 711533.

Dublin City Guide

PARKS AND GARDENS

Phoenix Park
Phoenix Park, covering over 1,760 acres, is the best-known park in Ireland. Enclosed by an 8-mile-long stone wall, the park was laid out in the mid-18thC and was the scene of the Phoenix Park murders in 1882, when the Chief Secretary and Under-Secretary for Ireland were assassinated. The park includes a number of buildings, the most important of which is Aras an Uachtarain; a private house built in 1751, it later became the house of the President of Ireland when Dr Douglas Hyde moved there in 1938. Other buildings are the houses of the Pope's ambassador and the American ambassador; St Mary's Hospital with handsome chapel by Thomas Cooley of 1771; the Magazine Fort of 1734. There is a racecourse at the north end, the people's gardens by the main entrance on Parkgate Street, and a zoo.

Zoological Gardens
The Zoological Gardens, inside Phoenix Park, are famous for the breeding of lions and other 'big cats'. The zoo has attractive gardens encircling two natural lakes where pelicans, flamingoes, ducks and geese abound.

National Botanic Gardens
Located in Glasnevin, it provides 50 acres of magnificent gardens with a fabulous collection of plants, shrubs and trees; established in 1790. Many of the plants come from tropical Africa and South America.

St Stephen's Green
In the heart of the city, St Stephen's Green was originally an open common enclosed in 1663. The earliest as well as the largest of Dublin's squares, it is encircled by magnificent 18thC and 19thC buildings, in particular No 85, by Richard Castle in 1739; No 86 by Robert West in 1765; on the west side, Nos 119–20 by Richard Castle and the Royal College of Surgeons by Edward Pike in 1806. The Green itself was opened to the general public in 1877.

St Anne's Park
St Anne's Park, to the north-east in Dollymount, is a large park covering over 270 acres and wooded with evergreen, oak, pine, beech, chestnut and lime. There is a lovely rose garden, opened in 1975. Formerly the house of the Guinness family.

Marley Park
Situated in Rathfarnham this large park contains areas of woodland, a large pond, nature trail and model railway.

ENTERTAINMENT, FOOD AND DRINK

CABARET
Braemor Rooms Churchtown. Tel: 988644.
Burlington Hotel Upper Leeson Street. Tel: 605222.
Jury's Hotel Ballsbridge. Tel: 605000.
Clontarf Castle Clontarf. Tel: 332321.
Abbey Tavern Howth. Tel: 390307.

RESTAURANTS
Celtic Mews Lower Baggot Street. Tel: 760796.
Ante Room Lower Baggot Street. Tel: 760796.
Johnny's Malahide Tel: 450314.
King Sitric Howth. Tel: 325235.
Le Coq Hardi Ballsbridge. Tel: 684130.
Lord Edward Christchurch. Tel: 752557.
Restaurant Na Mara Dun Laoghaire. Tel: 800509.
The Grey Door Upper Pembroke Street. Tel: 763286.
Guinea Pig Dalkey. Tel: 859055.
White's on the Green St Stephen's Green. Tel: 751975.
Old Dublin Francis Street. Tel: 751173.

PUBS AND CLUBS
Abbey Tavern (trad music) Howth. Tel: 390307.
Bailing, The Duke Street. Tel: 770600.
Black Lion Inn Emmet Road, Inchicore. Tel: 534580.
Bowes Fleet Street. Tel 714038.
Brazen Head Lower Brudge Street. Tel: 779549.
Davy Byrnes Duke Street. Tel: 711298.
Doheny and Nesbitts Lower Baggot Street. Tel: 762954.
Embankment City Saggart. Tel: 512032.
Gater Bar Lounge Crumlin Road. Tel: 540413.
Harp, The O'Connell Bridge. Tel: 776201.
Hourican Leeson Street. Tel: 762634.
Humphreys Ranelagh. Tel: 972490.
Kitty O'Shea's Grand Canal Street. Tel: 609965.
Long Hall Great George Street. Tel: 751590.

Dublin City Guide

Lough and Quay The Ninth Lock Clondalkin. Tel: 573268.
Madigans North Earl Street. Tel: 744613.
McDaids Harry Street. Tel: 794395.
Morrisseys Cork Street. Tel: 533286.
Mulligans Pollbeg Street. Tel: 775582.
O'Donoghues (trad music) Merrion Row. Tel: 762807.
Orchard Inn Killincarrig Delgany. Tel: 874631.
Palace Bar Fleet Street. Tel: 779290.
Ryans Parkgate. Tel: 776097.
Slattery's (trad music) Rathmines Road. Tel: 972052.
Stag's Head Dame Court. Tel: 793701.
Tamango Sands Hotel (night club) Port Marock. Tel: 460003.
Toner's Baggot Street. Tel: 763090.

THEATRES
Abbey Theatre Abbey Street Lower 1. Tel: 787222.
Dublin Resource Centre Crow Street. Tel: 771507.
Eblana Theatre Store Street 1. Tel: 746707.
Focus Theatre Pembroke Place, Pembroke Street 2. Tel: 763071.
Gaiety Theatre South King Street 2. Tel: 771717.
Gate Theatre Cavendish Row, Parnell Square. Tel: 744045.
Olympia Theatre 74 Dame Street 2. Tel: 778962.
Peacock Theatre Abbey Street Lower 1. Tel: 787222.
Players Theatre 3 Trinity College 2. Tel: 774673.
Project Arts Centre 39 East Essex Street. Tel: 713327.
SFX Centre Upper Sherrard Street 1. Tel: 741775.
The Studio 50 North Greater Georges Street 1. Tel: 962681.
John Player Theatre South Circular Road. Tel: 758445.
Lambert Puppet Theatre & Museum Clifton Lane, Monkstown. Tel: 800974.

CINEMAS
Adelphi Carlton Ltd 101 Abbey Street Middle 1. Tel: 732909.
Adelphi Cinema 98 Abbey Street Middle 1. Tel: 730433.
Ambassador Cinema O'Connell Street Upper 1. Tel: 727640.
Cameo Cinema Rere 52 Abbey Street Middle 1. Tel: 730249.
Carlton Cinema 52 Upper O'Connell Street 1. Tel: 731609.
Classic Cinema Harold's Cross Road 6. Tel: 975324.
Curzon Cinema 106 Abbey Street Middle 1. Tel: 730438.
Dublin Film Festival 1st Floor, 1 Suffolk Street 2. Tel. 792644.
Forum Cinema Dun Laoghaire. Tel: 809574.
Green Cinema St Stephen's Green 2. Tel: 751753.
Odeon Twin Cinemas 4 Eden Quay 1. Tel: 744611.
Ormonde Cinema Stillorgan Plaza, Stillorgan. Tel. 831144.
Savoy Cinema 19 O'Connell Street Upper 1. Tel: 748487.
Screen at College Townsend Street 2. Tel: 714988.
Stella Picture Theatre Ltd 207 Rathmines Road Lower 6. Tel: 971281.

PASSENGER TRAVEL

CAR FERRIES
Passenger and vehicle ferry services are:
British Rail 'Sealink' 15 Westmoreland Street, Dublin 2. Tel: 808844. Services: Dun Laoghaire–Holyhead, Rosslare–Fishguard, Larne–Stranraer.
B & I Line 16 Westmoreland Street, Dublin 2. Tel: 724711. Services: Dublin–Liverpool, Dublin–Holyhead, Rosslare–Fishguard, Dublin–Isle of Man.
Irish Continental Line 19–21 Aston Quay, Dublin 2. Tel: 774331. Services: Rosslare–Le Havre, Rossclare–Cherbourg.
Brittany Ferries Tourist House, 42 Grand Parade, Cork. Tel: (021) 507666. Services: Cork–Roscoff.

RAIL & BUS TRAVEL
Dublin is linked with the cities and towns of Ireland by a network of rail and bus services operated by Coras Iompair Eireann (CIE), which is Ireland's National Internal Transport Authority.

All information regarding rail and road services can be obtained from: CIE, 59 Upper O'Connell Street, Dublin 1. Tel: 787777.

Dublin City Guide

AIRLINES
Aer Arann Carnmore Airport, Galway. Tel: (091) 65119/65110.
Air Canada 4 Westmoreland Street, Dublin 2. Tel: (01) 771488.
Air France 29/30 Dawson Street, Dublin 2. Tel: (01) 778899.
Aer Lingus 40 Upper O'Connell Street, Dublin 1 and 42 Grafton Street, Dublin 2. Tel: (01) 377777.
British Airways 112 Grafton Street, Dublin 2. Tel: (01) 686666.
British Midland Airways Ltd Dublin Airport. Tel: (01) 373235.
Iberia Airlines of Spain Grafton Arcade, 3 Grafton Street, Dublin 2. Tel: (01) 774368 and 54 Dawson Street, Dublin 2. Tel: (01) 779846.
KLM Royal Dutch Airlines Hawkins House, Hawkins Street, Dublin 2. Tel: (01) 778241.
Lufthansa German Airlines Grattan House, 68/72 Lower Mount Street, Dublin 2. Tel: (01) 761595/6.
Ryanair 3 Dawson Street, Dublin 2. Tel: (01) 770444.
SAS Scandinavian Airlines Room 112, Link Building, Dublin Airport, Dublin. Tel: (01) 421922.
Sabena Belgian World Airlines 7 Dawson Street, Dublin 2. Tel: (01) 716677.
Swissair Swiss Transport Co Ltd 54 Dawson Street, 3rd Floor, Dublin 2. Tel: (01) 712197/778173.

HOTELS
Ashling Parkgate Street. Tel: 772324.
Berkeley Court Lansdowne Road. Tel: 601711.
Burlington Leeson Street. Tel: 605222.
Buswells Molesworth Street. Tel: 764013.
Fitzpatricks Castle Killiney. Tel: 851533.
Green Isle Naas Road, Clondalkin. Tel: 593406.
Gresham Upper O'Connell Street. Tel: 746881.
International Airport Dublin Airport. Tel: 379211.
Jury's Ballsbridge. Tel: 605000.
Montrose Stillorgan Road. Tel: 693311.
Mount Herbert Herbert Road. Tel: 684321.
Royal Dublin O'Connell Street. Tel: 733666.
Sands Coast Road, Portmarnock. Tel: 460003.
Shelbourne St Stephen's Green. Tel: 766471.
Skylon Drumcondra Road. Tel: 379121.
Spa Lucan. Tel: 280494.
Tara Towers Merrion Road. Tel: 694666.
Westbury Clarendon Street. Tel: 791122.

SHOPPING
DEPARTMENT STORES
Arnott's Henry Street. Tel: 721111.
Switzers Grafton Street. Tel: 776821.
Roches Stores Henry Street. Tel: 730044.
Brown Thomas Grafton Street. Tel: 776861.
Clery and Co O'Connell Street. Tel: 786000.

SUPERMARKET CHAINS
There are several branches of each of the following supermarkets in Dublin: Quinnsworth, Superquinn, Dunnes Stores and Shopping Baskets.

BOOKSHOPS
Bookhouse Ireland Tel: 934733.
Eason & Son Ltd Lower O'Connell Street. Tel: 733811.
Greene & Co Clare Street. Tel: 762554.
Alan Hanna Bookshop Rathmines. Tel: 967398.
Fred Hanna Ltd Nassau Street. Tel: 771255.
Hodges Figgis Dawson Street. Tel: 774754.
Paperback Centre Suffolk Street. Tel: 774210.
Paperback Centro Stillorgan Shopping Centre. Tel: 886341.
Book Stop Dun Laoghaire Shopping Centre. Tel: 809917.
Book Stop Blackrock Shopping Centre. Tel: 832193.
Book Shop Rathfarnham Shopping Centre. Tel: 934733.
Books Unlimited Donaghmede Shopping Centre. Tel: 470952.
Eason Ilac Centre Mary Street. Tel: 721322.
Eason Irish Life Centre Talbot Street. Tel: 727010.
Parsons Bookshop Baggot Street. Tel: 603616.
Rainbow Bookshop Nutgrove. Tel: 932957.
Waterstone's Dawson Street. Tel: 791260.
Geo. Webb Crampton Quay. Tel: 777489.

Dublin City Guide

Dundrum Bookshop Main Street, Dundrum. Tel: 987334.
Bray Bookshop Quinsboro Road, Bray. Tel: 862786.
Eason Dun Laoire Georges Street. Tel: 805528.

MARKETS
Iveagh Market (old clothes, furniture, etc) Francis Street.
Liberty Market (clothes, fabrics, household goods) Meath Street.
Moore Street Market (fruit and vegetables) off Henry Street.
Vegetable Market (fruit, vegetables, fish and flowers) St Michan's Street.

SPORTS VENUES

Athletics (International Venue)
Croke Park GAA — Tel: 363222.

Angling
Irish Angling Association — Tel: 379206.

Bathing, Beaches
There are safe sandy beaches at:
Dollymount — 3½ miles from Dublin.
Claremount — 9 miles from Dublin.
Sutton — 7 miles from Dublin.
Portmarnock — 9 miles from Dublin.
Donabate — 13 miles from Dublin.
Malahide — 9 miles from Dublin.

Baths (indoor, heated)
For full details tel: 776811 Ext 189/190.
Ballyfermot — Le Fanu Park.
Ballymun — Seven Tower Shopping Centre.
Coolock — Northside Shopping Centre.
Crumlin — Windmill Road.
Finglas — Mellowes Road.
Iveagh Baths — Bride Street.
Rathmines — Williams Park.
Sean McDermott Street — City Centre.
There are outdoor swimming baths, open from June to September, at:
Blackrock, Dun Laoghaire, Clontarf.

Bowling Centres
Dundrum Bowl — Sandyford Road, Dundrum 14. Tel: 980209.
Stillorgan Bowl — Stillorgan. Tel: 881656.

Flying
Weston Aerodrome — Celbridge Road, Lucan. Tel: 280435.

Football (International Venue)
Dalymount Park — Tel: 300923.

Golf
18-hole golf clubs:
Beech Park — 10 miles from Dublin.
Castle Golf Club — Rathfarnham, 4 miles from Dublin.
Clontarf Golf Club — 2½ miles from Dublin.
Donabate — 13 miles from Dublin.
Forrest Little Golf Club — 5½ miles from Dublin.
Dun Laoghaire — 7 miles from Dublin.
Edmonstown — 6 miles from Dublin.
Elm Park — 3½ miles from Dublin.
Grange Rathfarnham — 6 miles from Dublin.
Hermitage Lucan — 7¼ miles from Dublin.
Howth — 9 miles from Dublin.
Island Malahide — 9 miles from Dublin.
Milltown — 4½ miles from Dublin.
Newlands Clondalkin — 6 miles from Dublin.
Portmarnock — 9 miles from Dublin.
Royal Dublin — Dollymount, 3 miles from Dublin.
Woodbrook — near Bray, 11½ miles from Dublin.
Slade Valley — Saggart, 9 miles from Dublin.
Stackstown — 9 miles from Dublin.

Greyhound Racing
Greyhound racing is one of Ireland's leading spectator sports. Meetings are held at:
Shelbourne Park Stadium — Ringsend (Mon, Wed and Sat at 8 pm).
Harolds Cross Stadium — (Tues, Thur and Fri at 8 pm).

Horse Racing
There are three racecourses on the outskirts of Dublin:
Phoenix Park — 3 miles from Dublin.
Leopardstown — 6 miles from Dublin.
Fairyhouse — 12 miles from Dublin.

Ice Skating
Dublin Ice Rink — Dolphins Barn. Tel: 532170.

Leisure Centre (various sports)
Ballyfermot — Tel: 264648.

Rugby (International Venue)
Lansdowne Road — Tel: 689292.

Sports Clubs
Amateur Football League — Tel: 483777.
Badminton Hall — Tel: 505966.
Ballyboden/St Edna's GAA — Tel: 947950.

Dublin City Guide 17

Blackrock RFC — Tel: 805967.
Castleknock Lawn Tennis Club — Tel: 210423.
Clontarf Cricket & Football Club — Tel: 336214.
Clontarf Yacht & Boat Club — Tel: 332691.
Craobh Chiarain GAA — Tel: 311050.
Cuala Chiarain GAA — Tel: 850783.
Crumlin Bowling Club — Tel: 558141.
Garda Boat Club — Tel: 770127.
Irish Rowing Union — Tel: 962608.
Irish Hang Gliding Club — Tel: 04045726.
Irish Kennel Club — Tel: 758126.
Irish Lawn Tennis Association — Tel: 606332.
Irish Parachute Club — Tel: 719511.
Junior Chamber — Tel: 714387.
Kilternan Tennis Centre — Tel: 953720.
Lansdowne Football Club — Tel: 689300.
Neptune Rowing Club — Tel: 775079.
Pierrot Snooker (Shelb) Club — Tel: 680500.
Polo Club — Tel: 776248.
Regal Diplomat Snooker Club — Tel: 202232.
St Mary's College RFC — Tel: 900440.
Ski Club of IRE — Tel: 955658.
St Brigids GAA — Tel: 202484.
Stackstown Golf Club — Tel: 942338.
Sutton Lawn Tennis — Tel: 233035.
Terenure RFC — Tel: 907572.
Vocational Schools Sports — Tel: 905981.
St Vincent's Hurling & Football Club — Tel: 311116.
Stock Car Racing — Old Airport Road, Santry (April–Sept, every Sunday at 3.30 pm. Tel: 318448).

HELP & ADVICE

SOCIAL SERVICE AND WELFARE ORGANISATIONS
Adoption Board Tel: 762004.
Aid Parents Under Stress Tel: 788344.
Alcoholics Anonymous Tel: 977656.
Asthma Society of Ireland Tel: 716551.
Dr Barnardos Tel: 977276.
Central Remedial Clinic Tel: 332626.
Cherish Tel: 682744.
Dublin Central Mission Tel: 742123.
Rape Crisis Centre Tel: 614911.
Irish Epilepsy Association Tel: 516500.

Irish Heart Foundation Tel: 685001.
Irish Red Cross Tel: 765135.
Irish Society for Prevention of Cruelty to Children Tel: 761293.
Irish Wheelchair Association Tel: 338533.
National Association for the Deaf Tel: 763118.
National Council for the Blind. Tel: 612032.
Rehabilitation Institute Tel: 698422.
Samaritans Tel: 778833.
St Vincent De Paul Tel: 542181.

HOSPITALS
St Vincents Elm Park. Tel: 694533.
St Michaels Lower George Street, Dun Laoghaire. Tel: 806901.
St Michaels (Pte), Crofton Road, Dun Laoghaire. Tel: 808411.
James Connolly Blanchardstown. Tel: 213844.
Jervis Street Tel: 723355.
St Laurence's (Richmond), North Brunswick Street. Tel: 721666.
Mater Misericordiae Eccles Street. Tel: 301122.
St James James Street. Tel: 532867.
Beaumont Beaumont Road. Tel: 377755.

GARDA SIOCHANA (POLICE)
Dublin Metropolitan Area Headquarters, Harcourt Square. Tel: 732222.

EMBASSIES
American Tel: 688777.
Apostolic Nunciature Tel: 309344.
Arab Republic of Egypt Tel: 606566.
Australian Tel: 761517.
British Tel: 695211.
Canadian Tel: 781988.
French Tel: 694777.
German Tel: 693011.
Italian Tel: 601744.
Spanish Tel: 691640.
USSR Tel: 979525.

CAR REPAIRS
Annesley Motor Company Ballybough. Tel: 723033.
Brady's (Dublin) Ltd Navan Road, Castleknock. Tel: 213053.
Carroll and Kinsella Motors Western Industrial Estate. Tel: 516622.
Parkgate Motors Parkgate Street. Tel: 775677.

18 Key to Map Pages

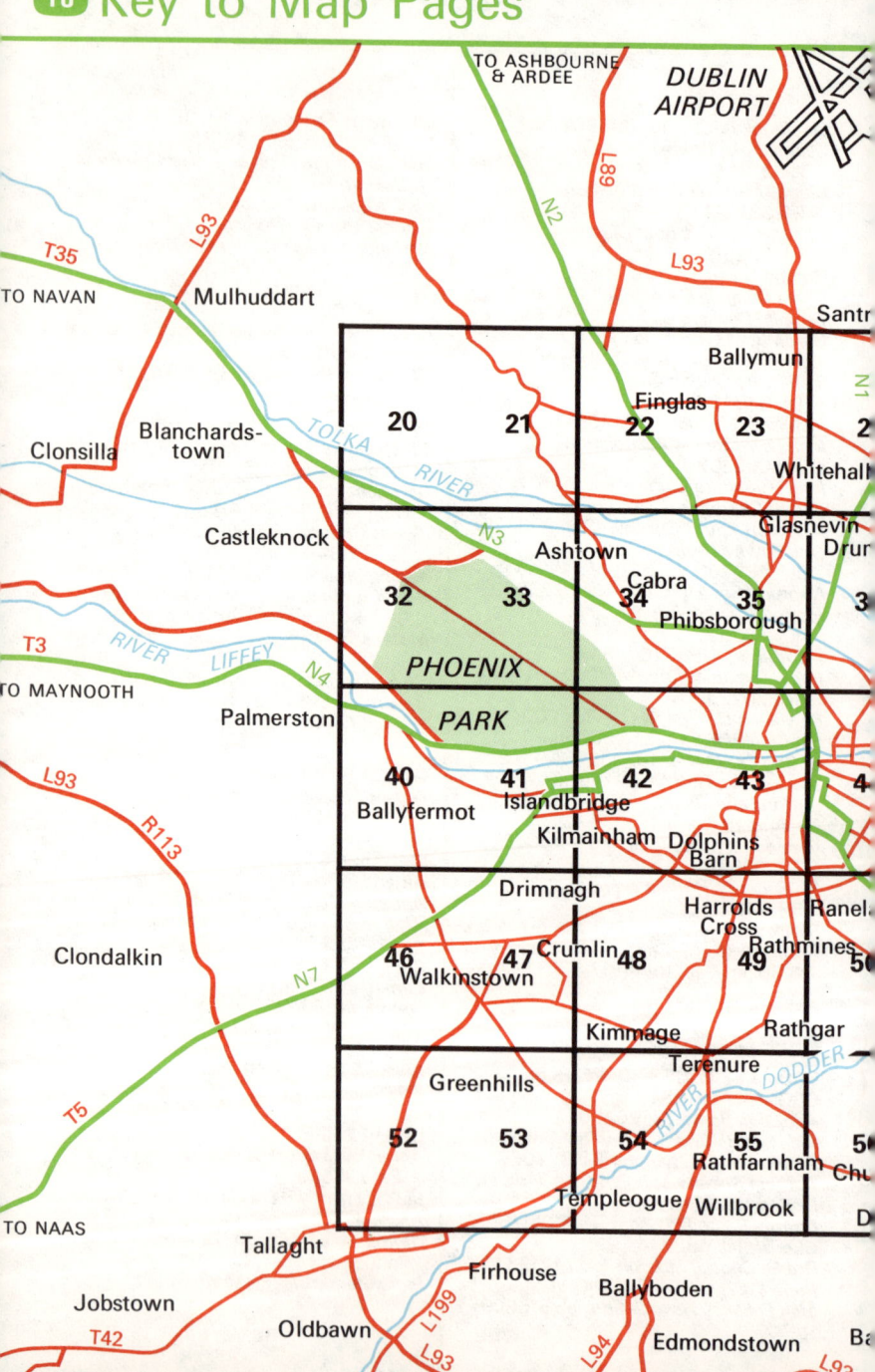

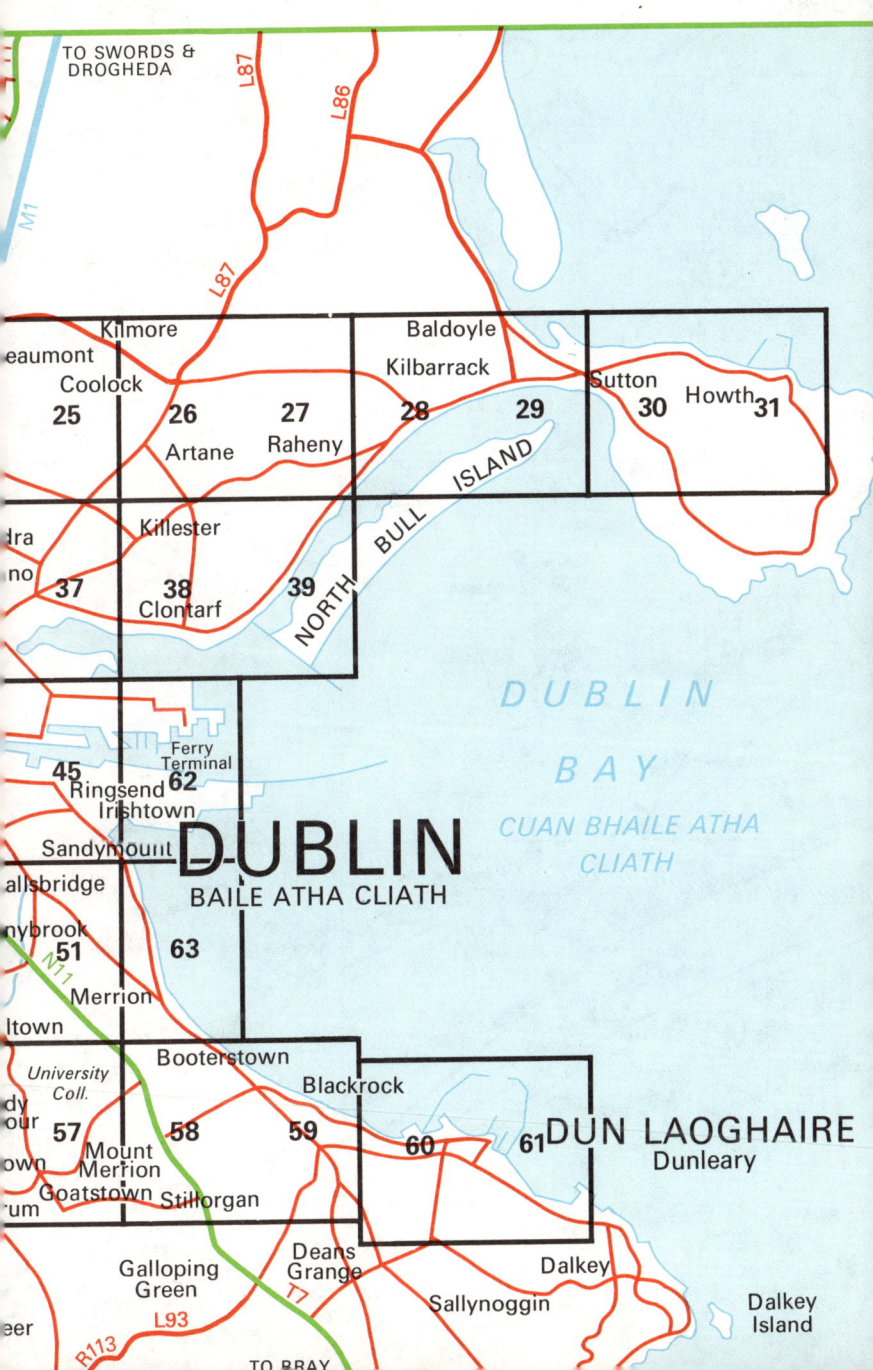

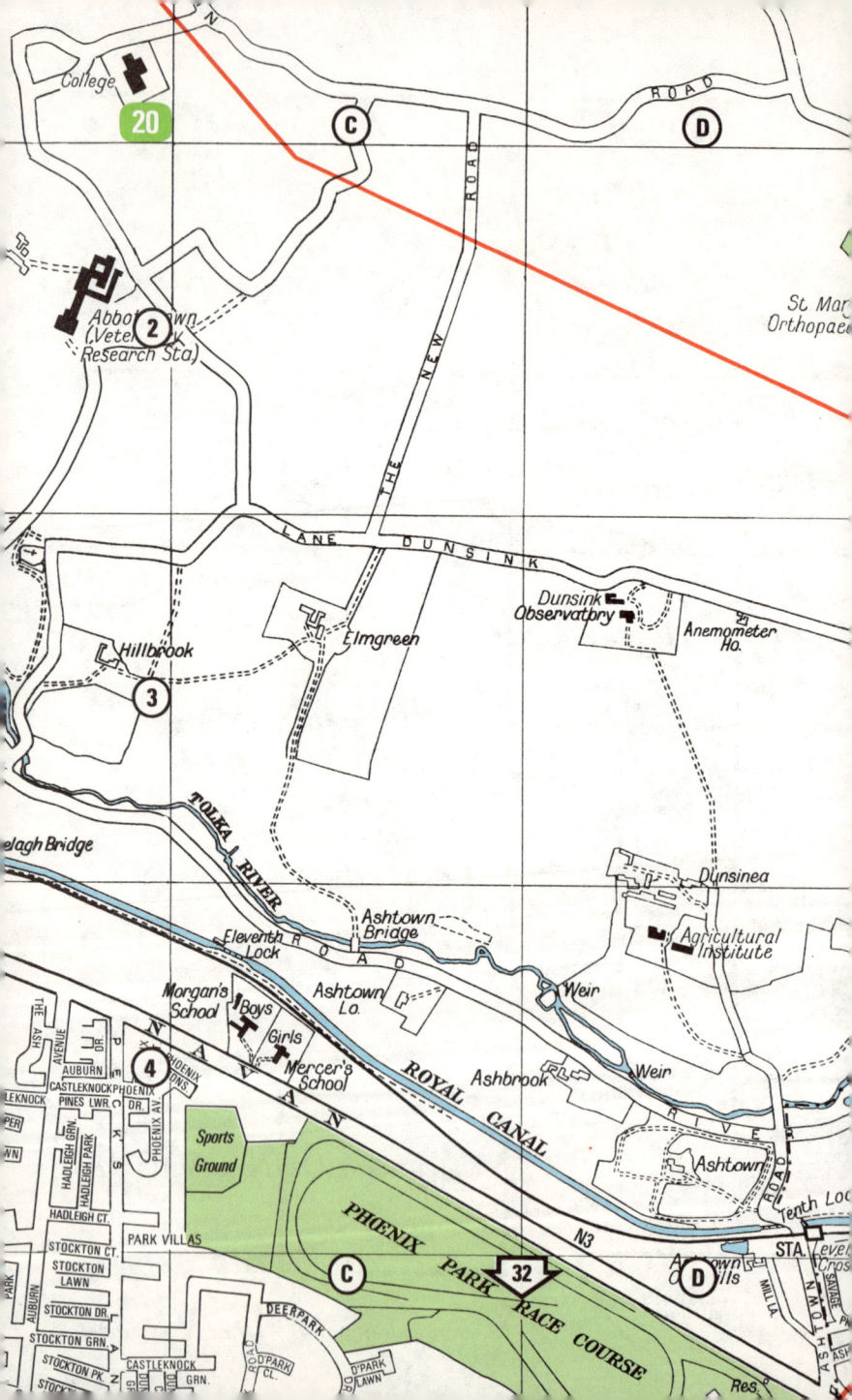

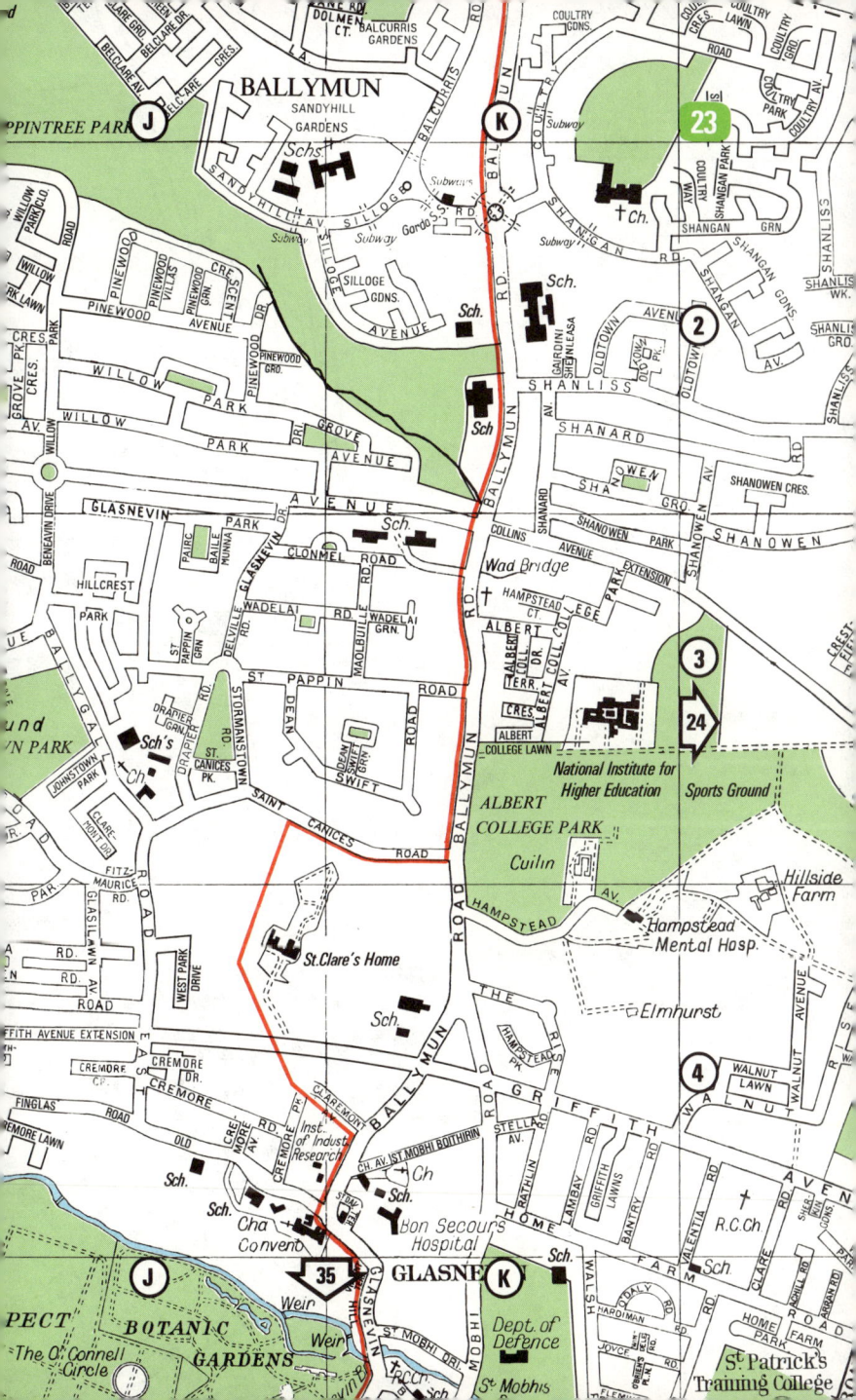

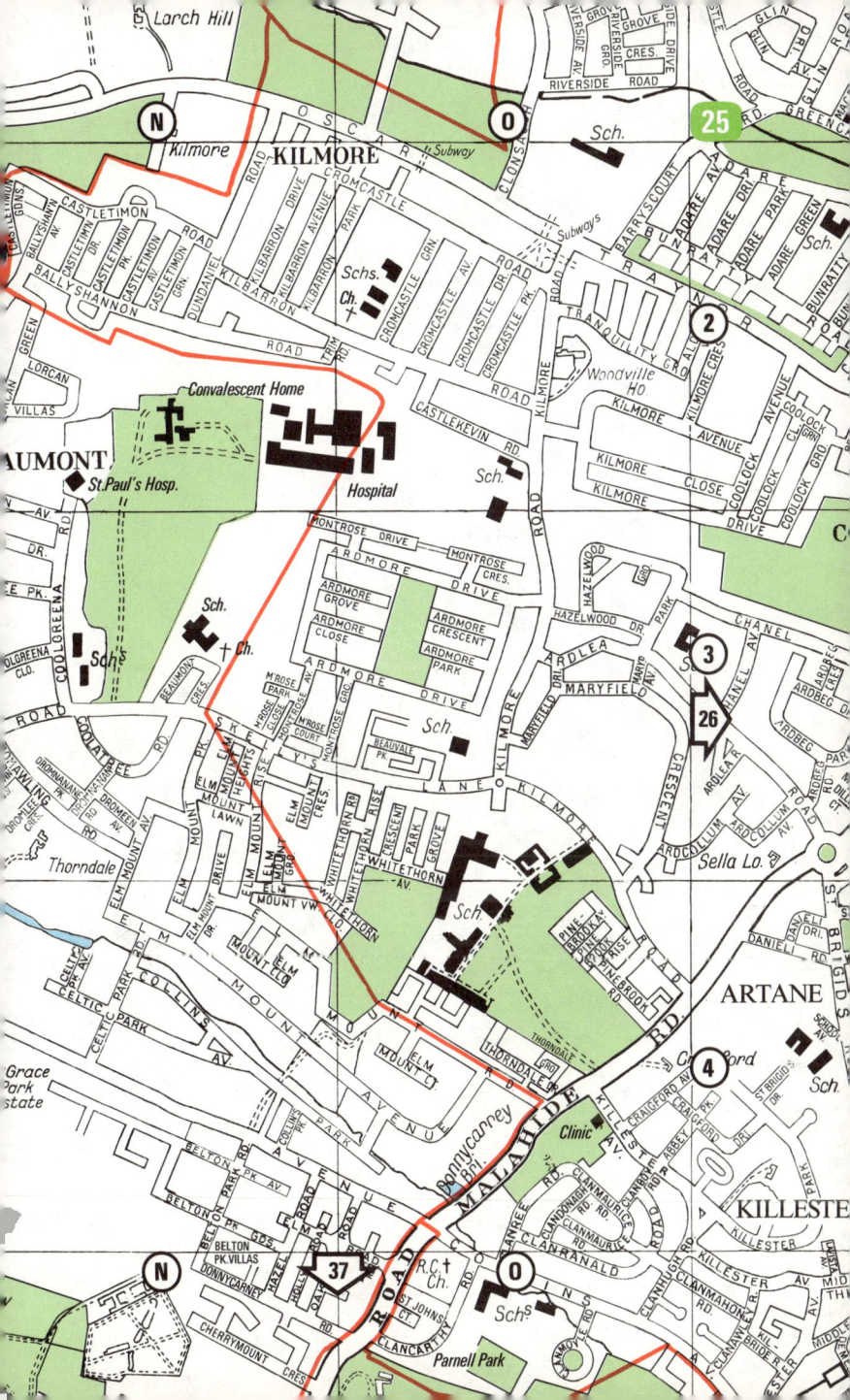

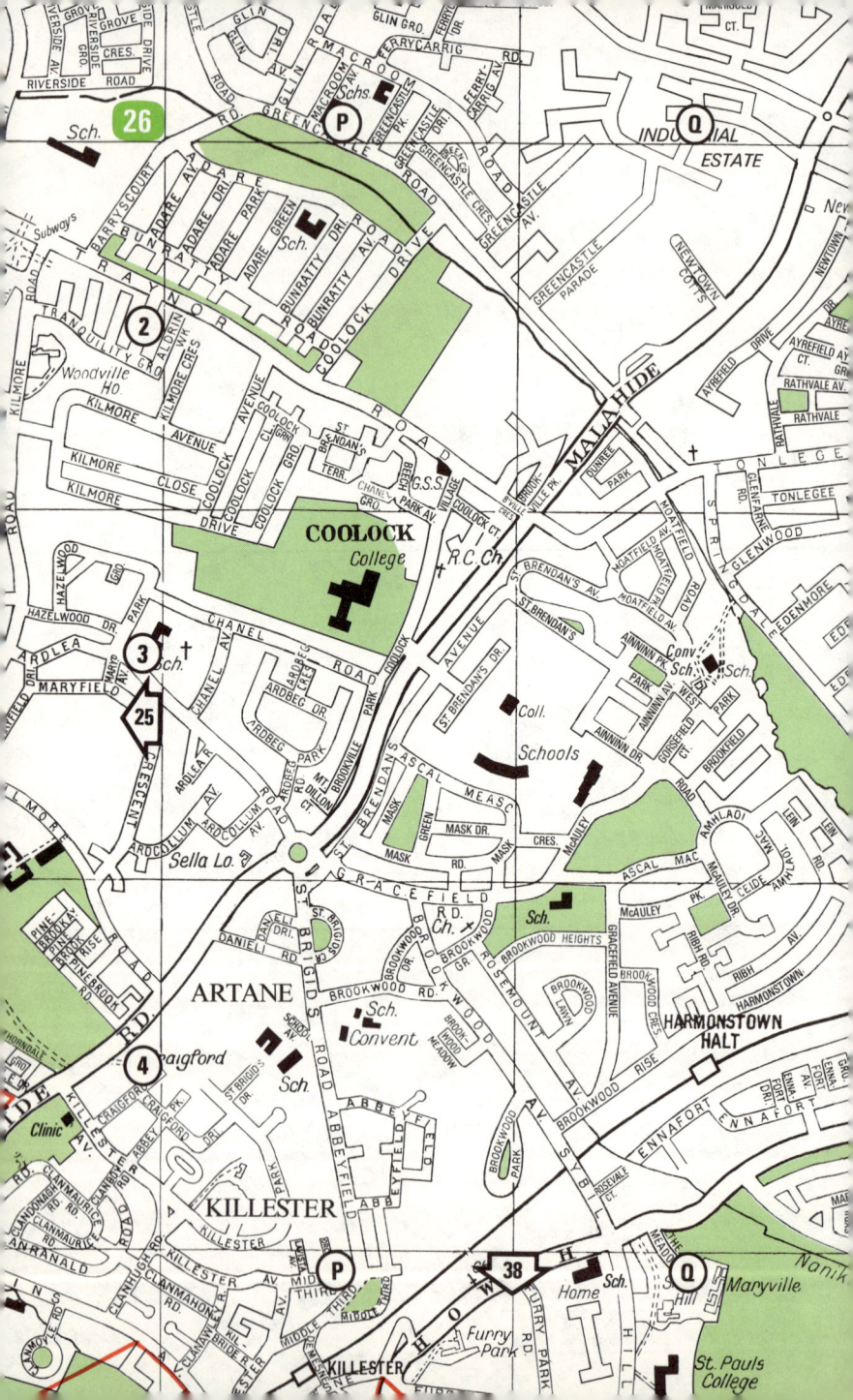

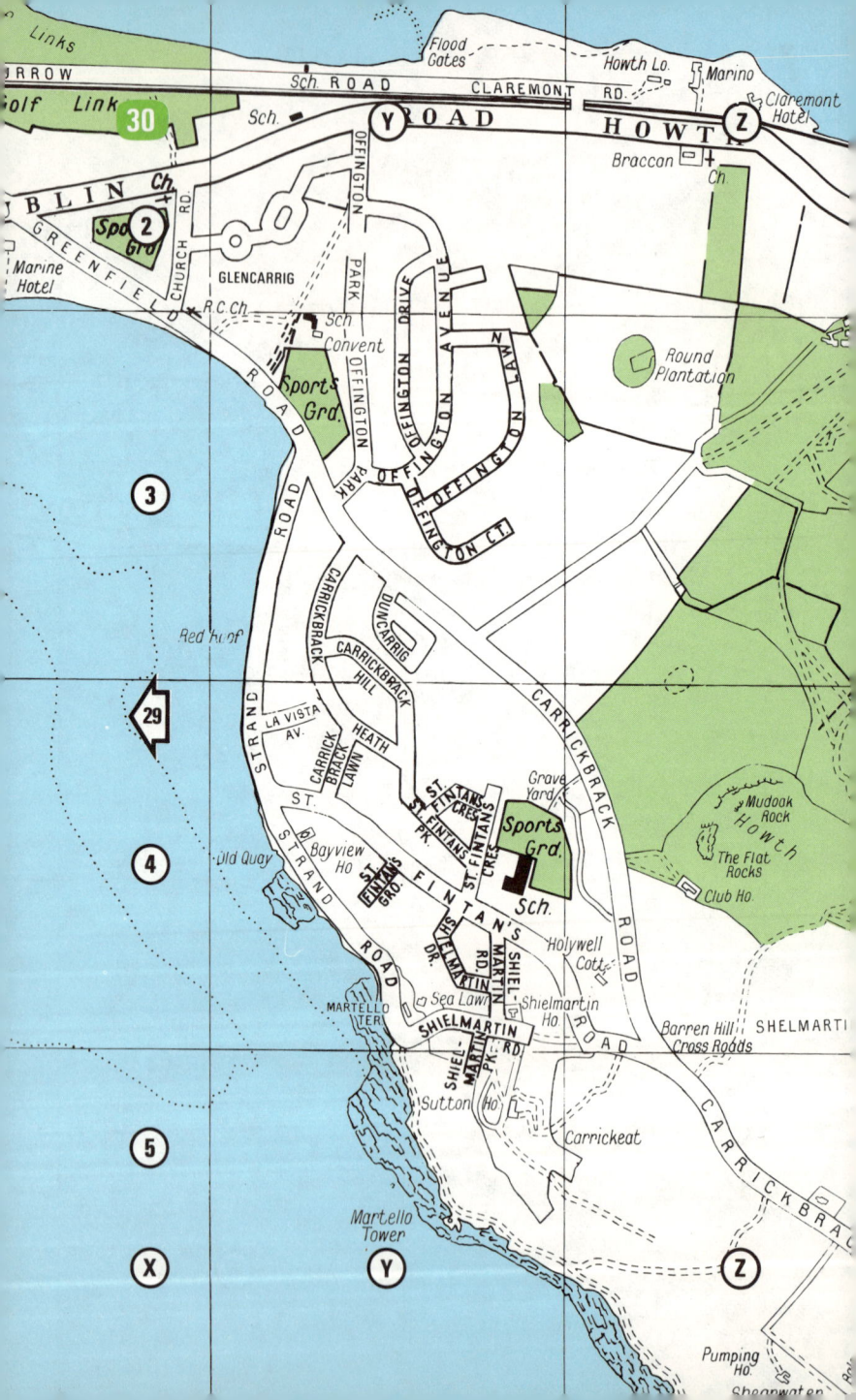

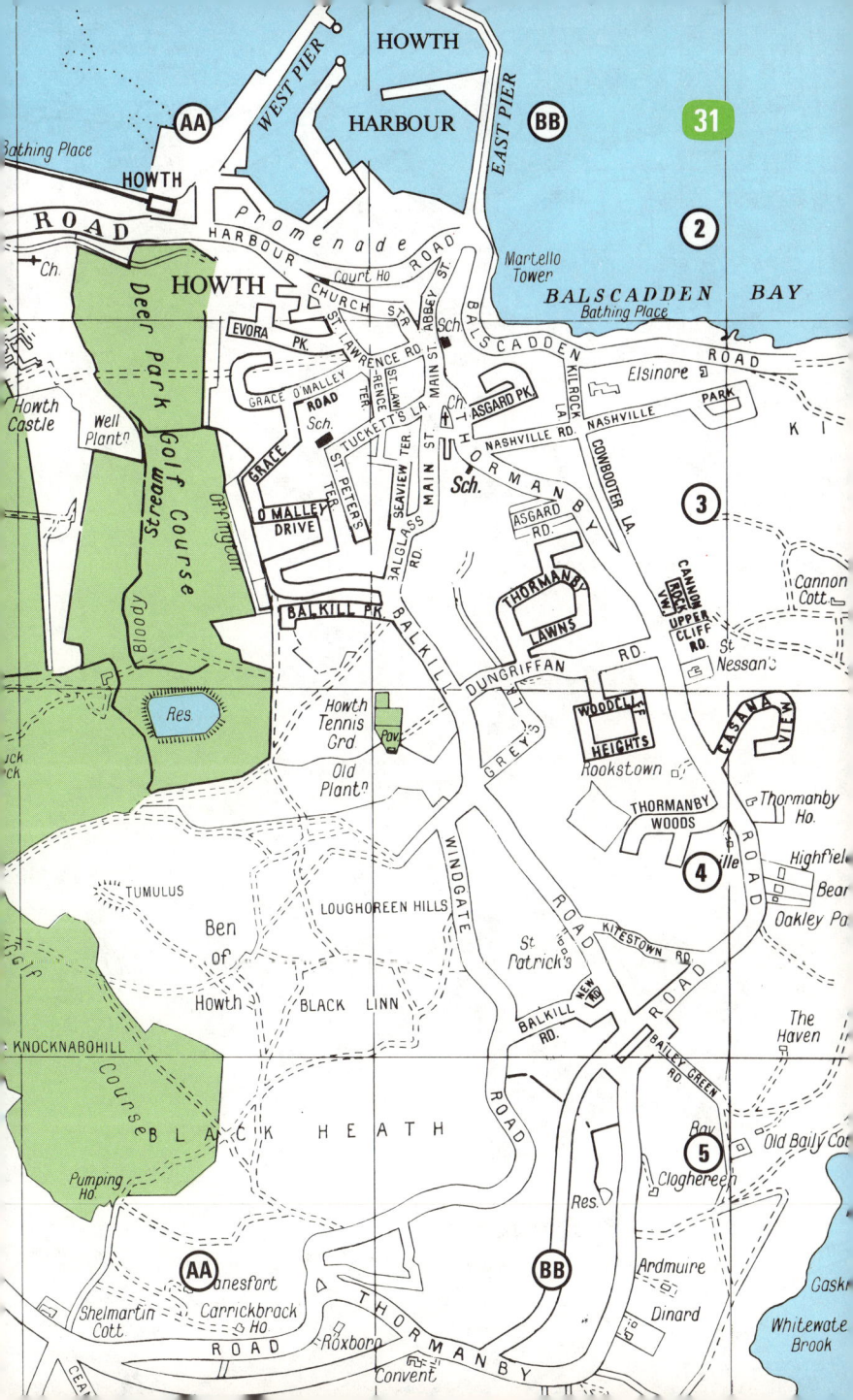

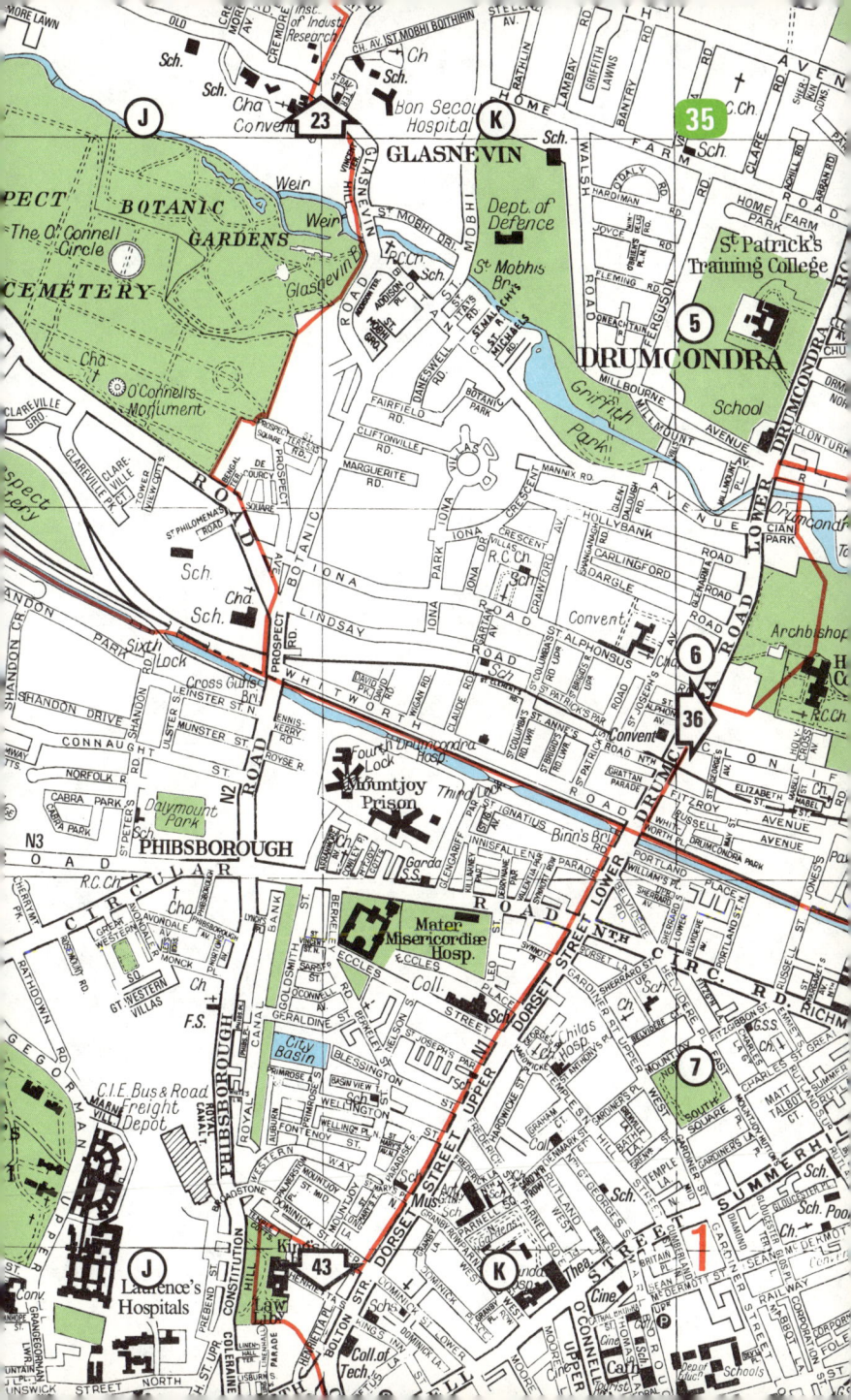

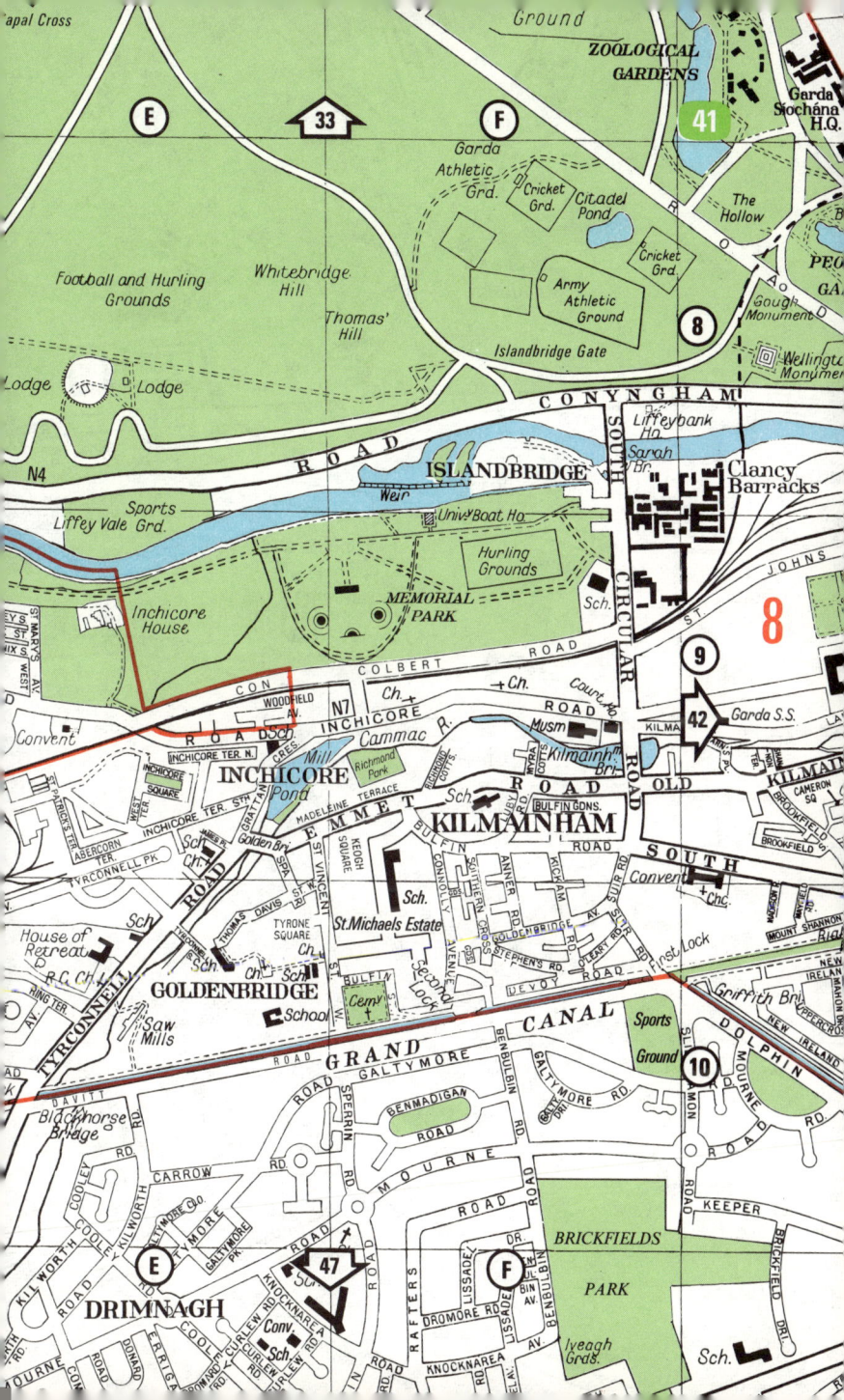

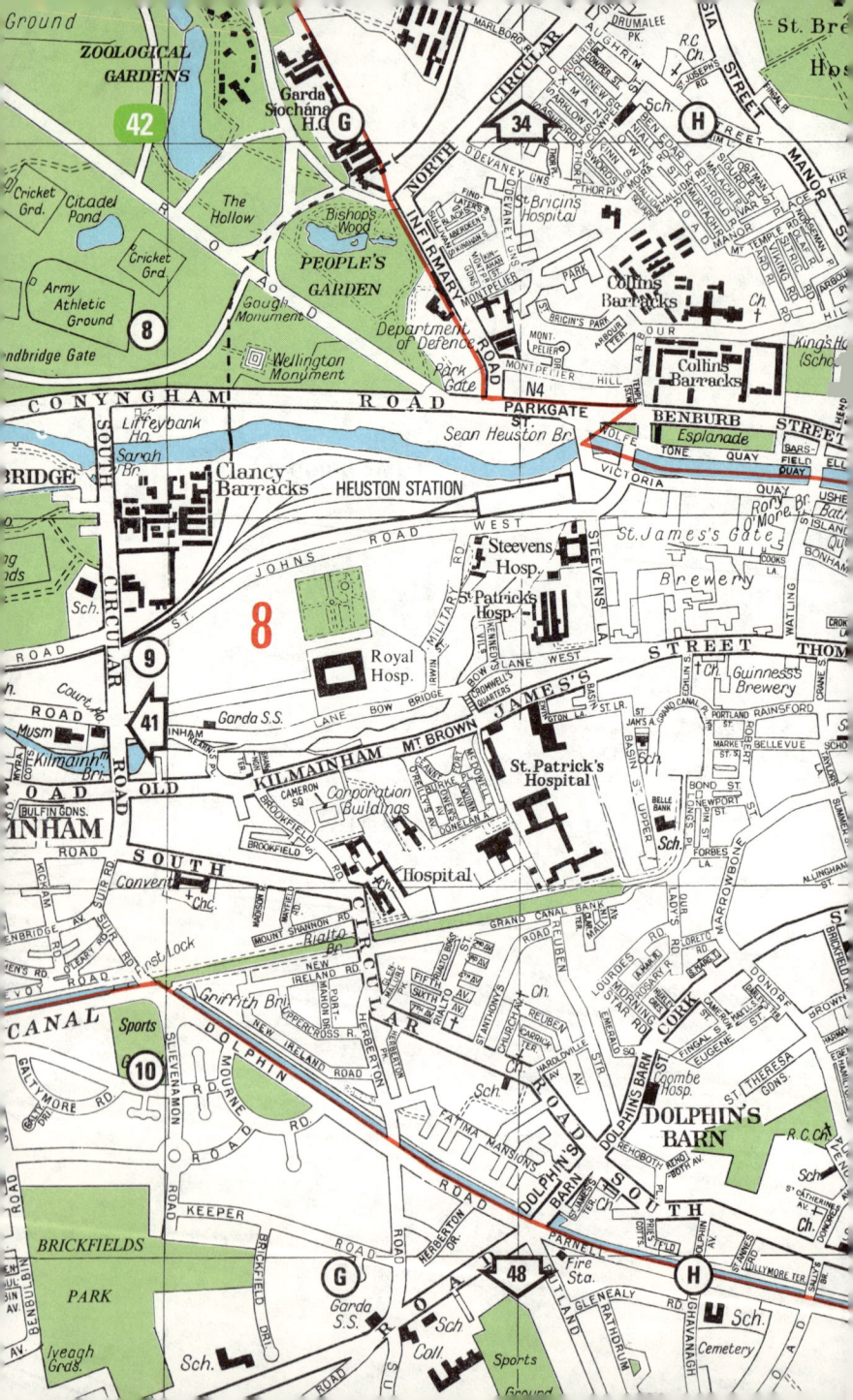

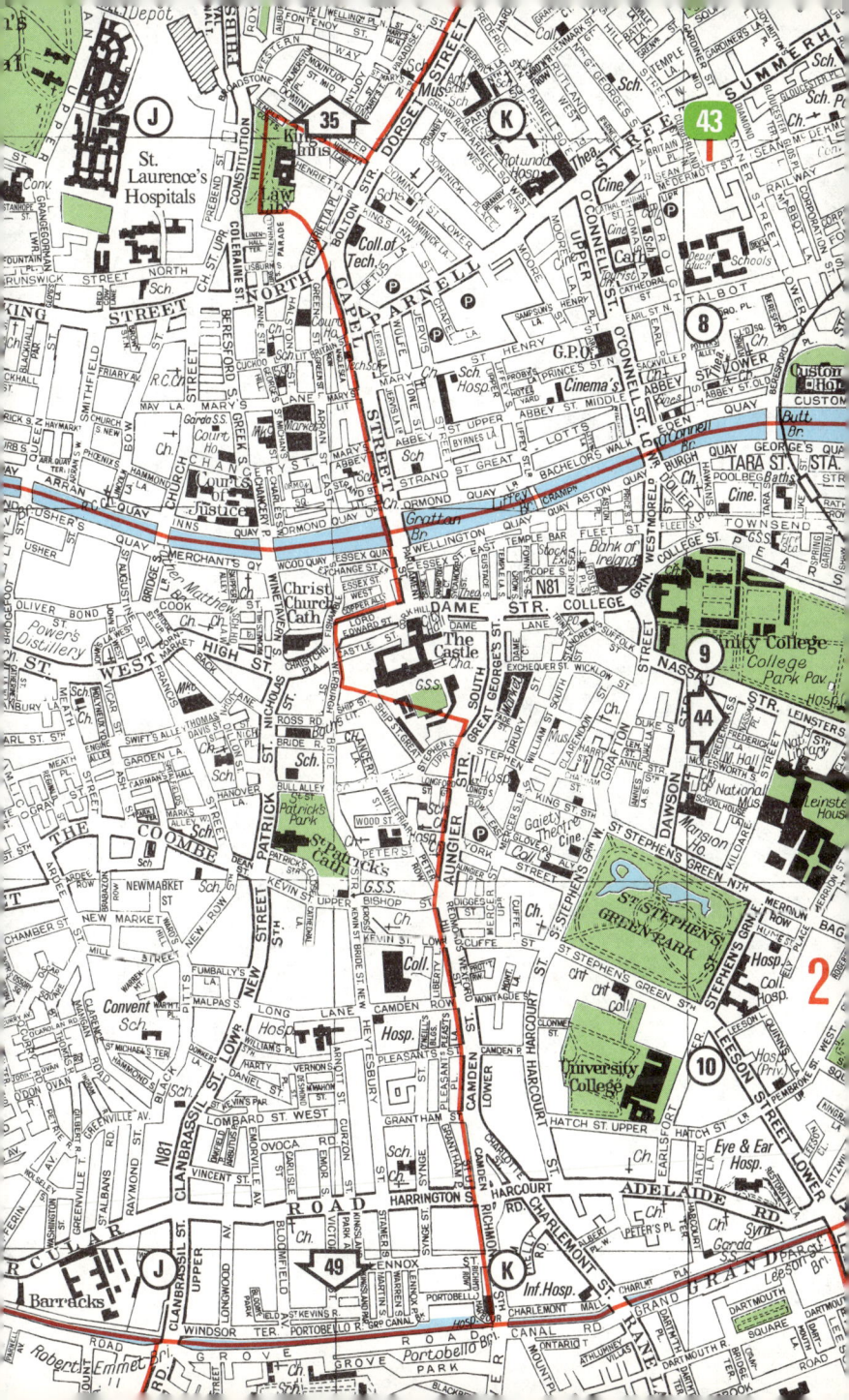

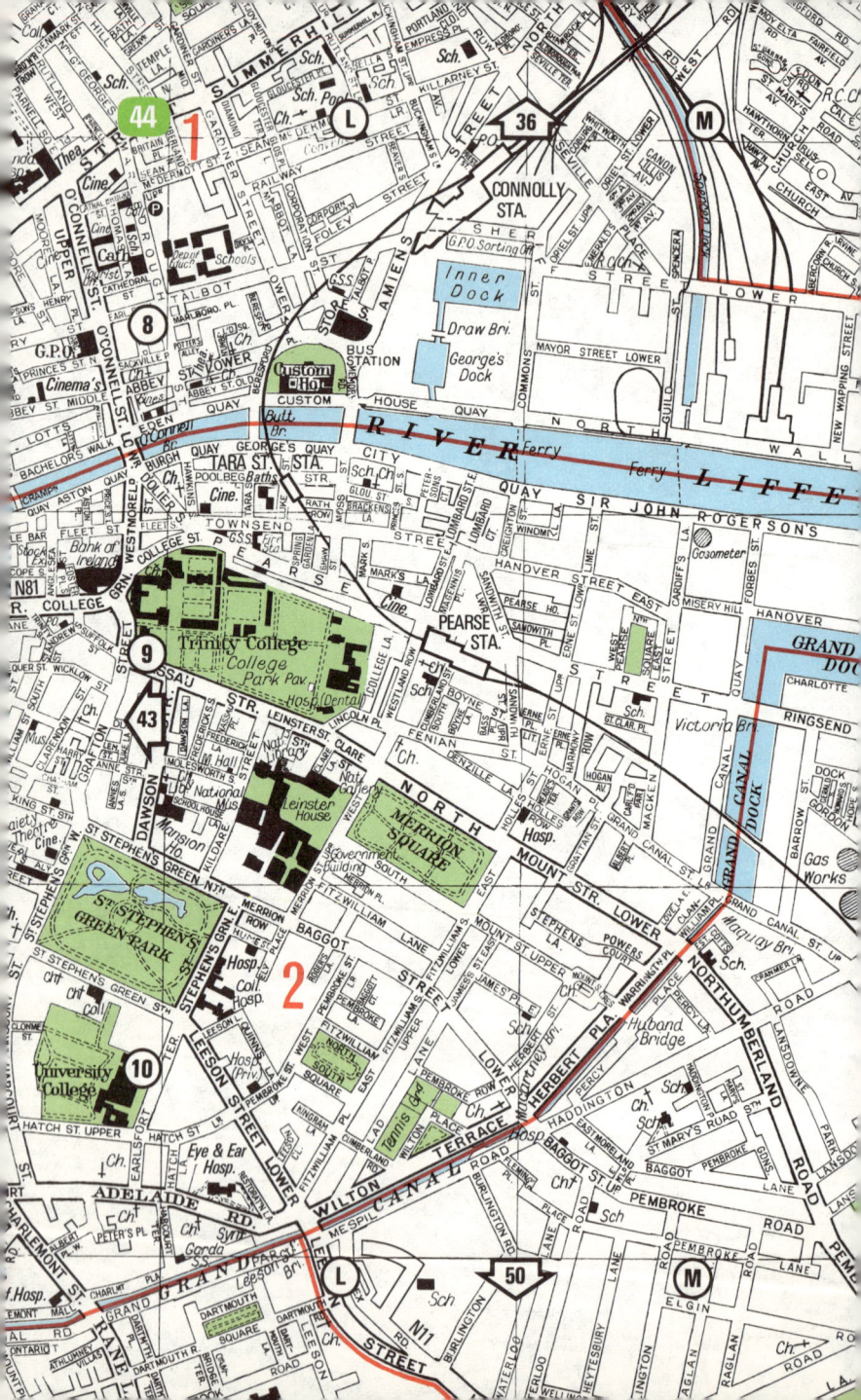

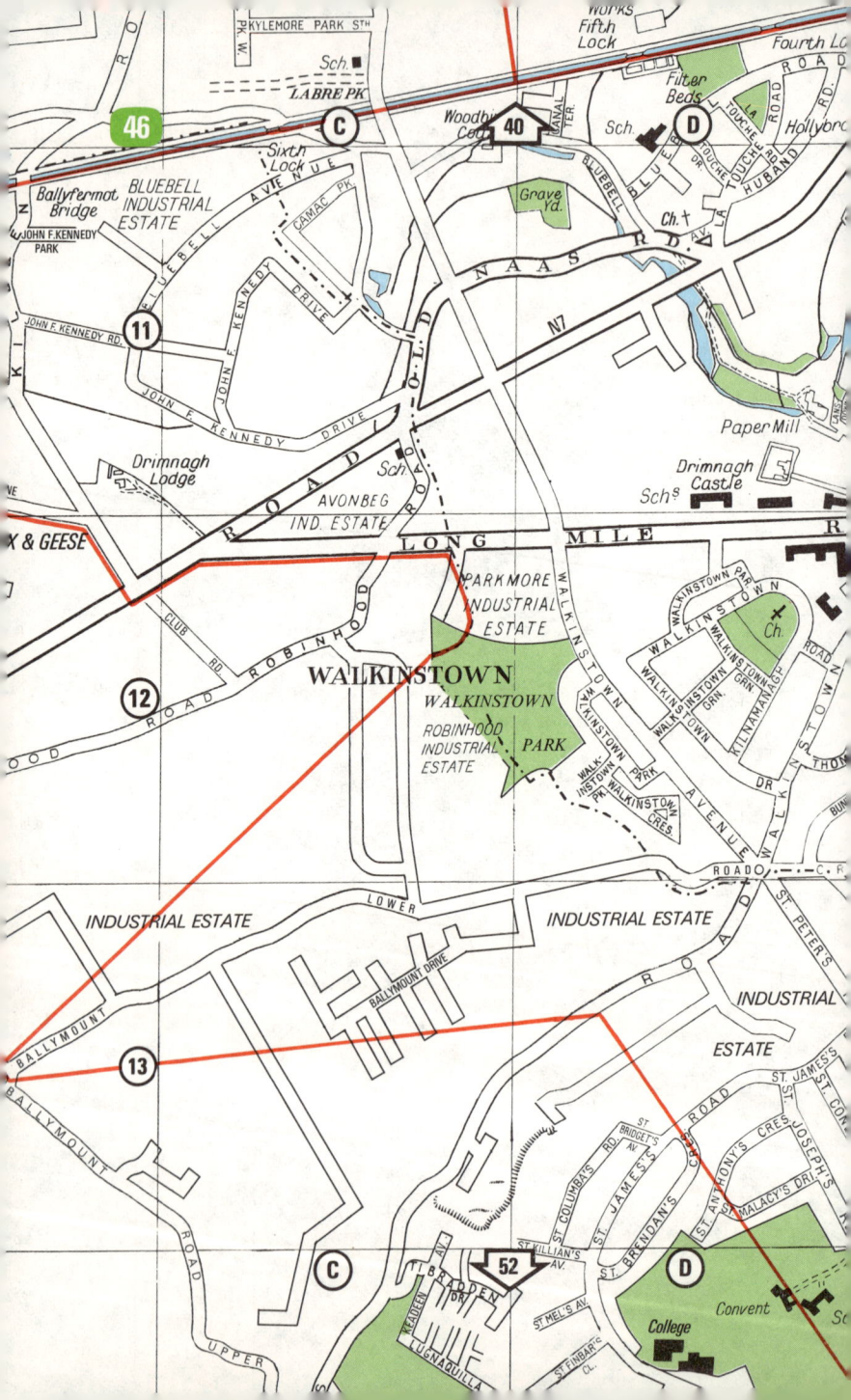

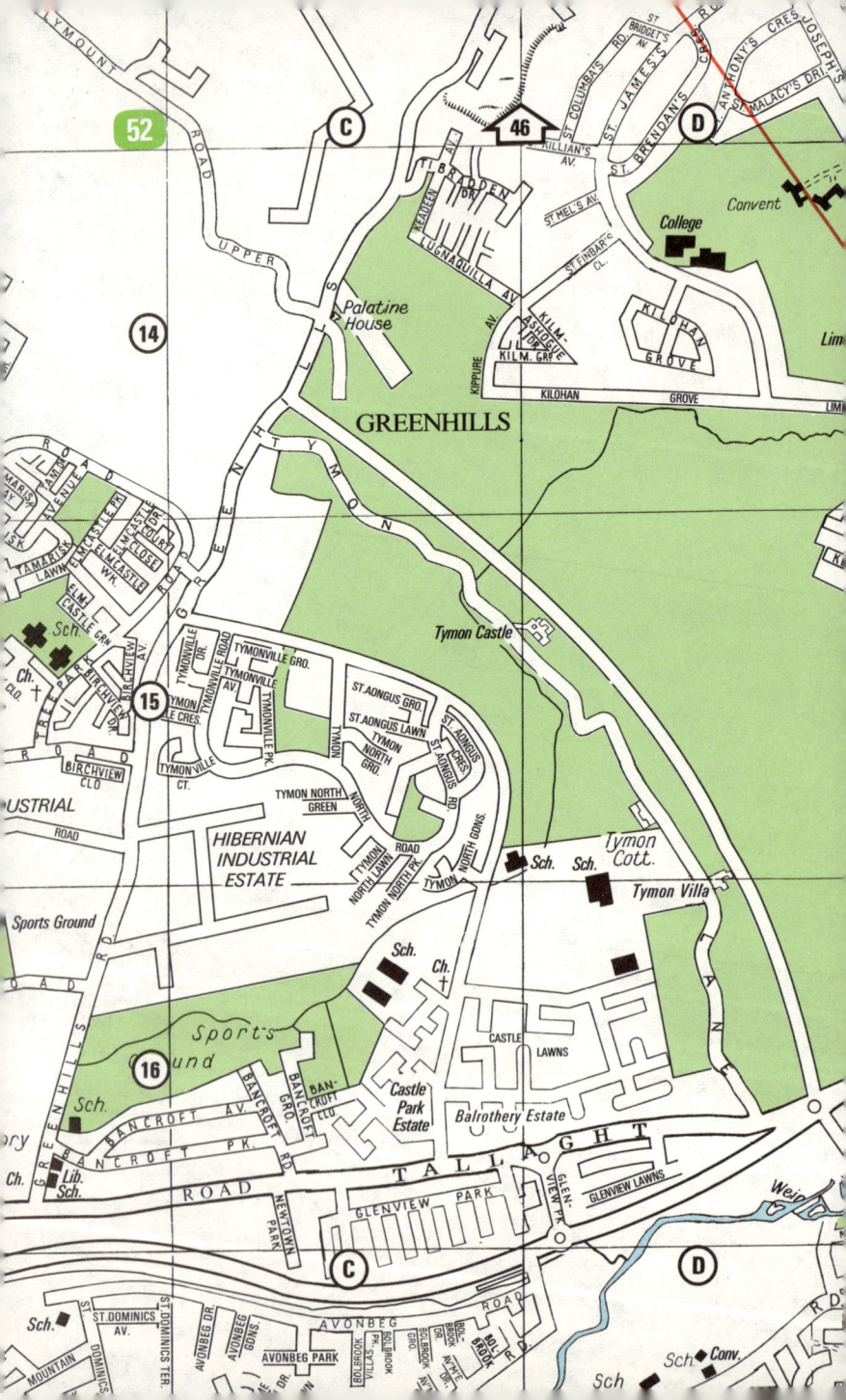

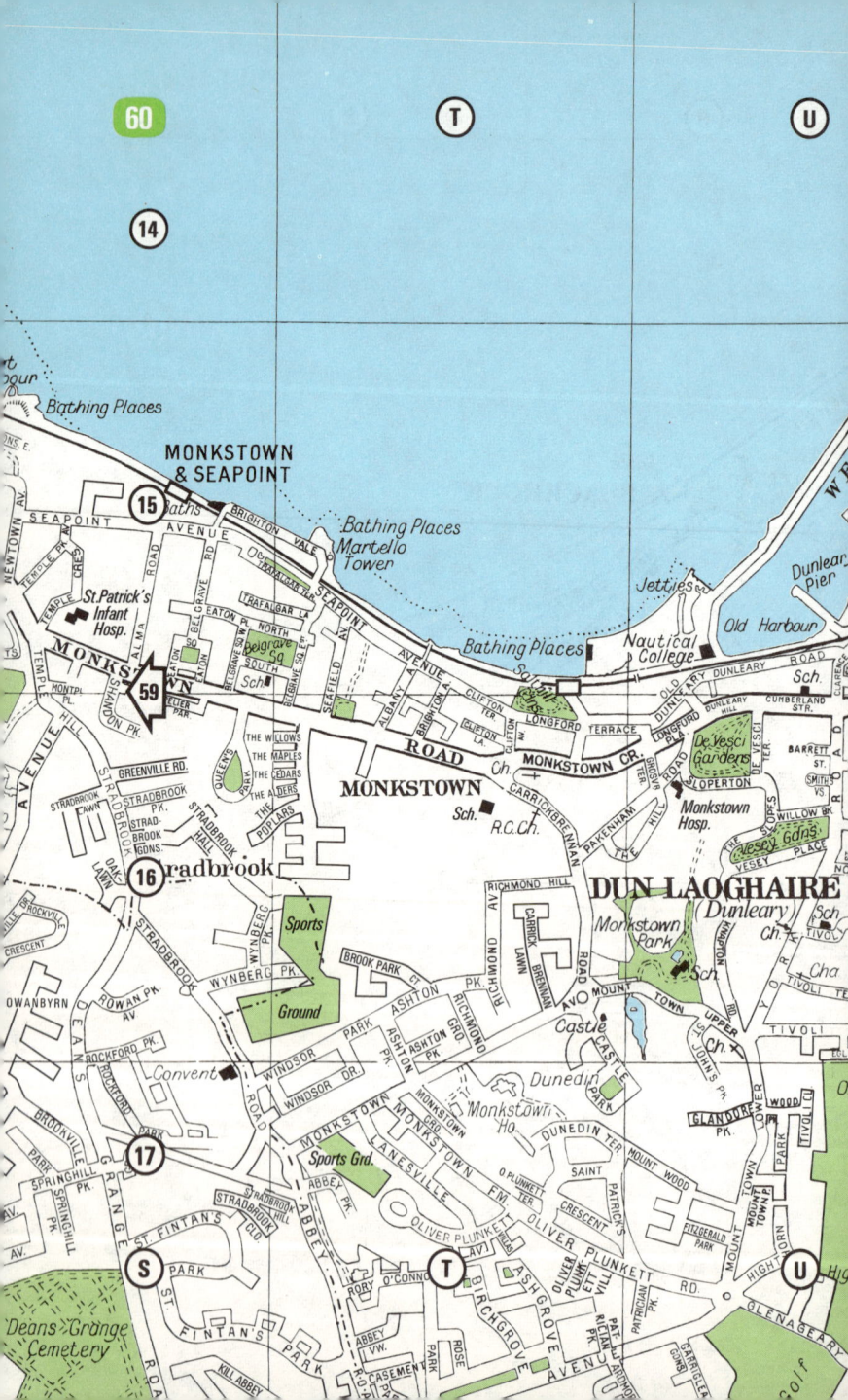

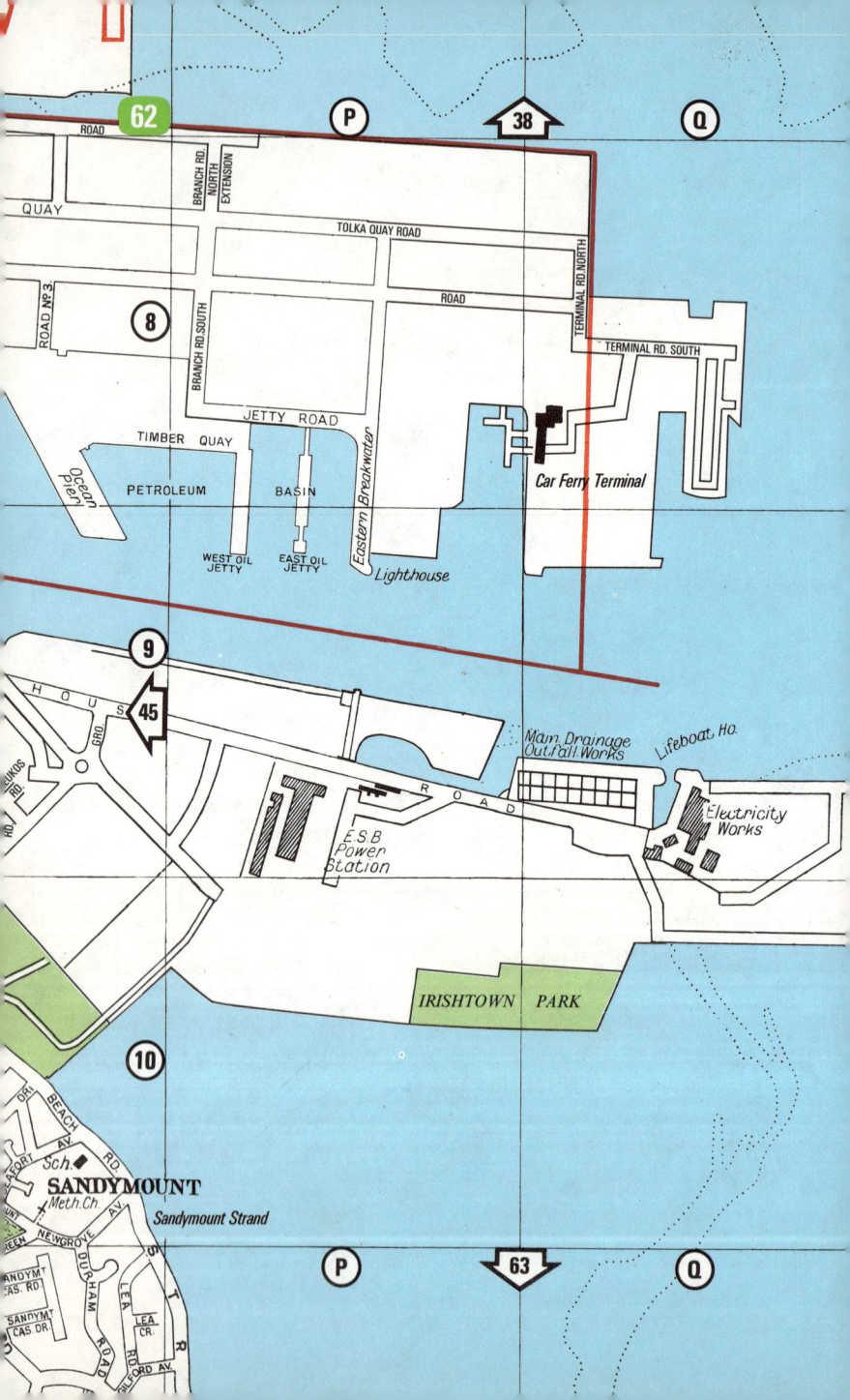

INDEX TO GEOGRAPHIA STREET ATLAS OF DUBLIN

General Abbreviations

All.	Alley	Cor.	Corner	Grn.	Green	N.	North	Sq.	Square
App.	Approach	Cotts.	Cottages	Gro.	Grove	Par.	Parade	Sta.	Station
Arc.	Arcade	Cres.	Crescent	Ho.	House	Pass.	Passage	St.	Street
Av.	Avenue	Ct.	Court	Ind.	Industrial	Pk.	Park	Ter.	Terrace
Bldgs.	Buildings	Dr.	Drive	La.	Lane	Pl.	Place	Vills.	Villas
Boul.	Boulevard	E.	East	Lo.	Lodge	Prom.	Promenade	Vw.	View
Bri.	Bridge	Est.	Estate	Mans.	Mansions	Quad.	Quadrant	W.	West
Circ.	Circus	Esp.	Esplanade	Mkt.	Market	Ri.	Rise	Wf.	Wharf
Cft.	Croft	Gdns.	Gardens	Ms.	Mews	Rd.	Road	Wk.	Walk
Clo	Close	Gra.	Grange	Mt.	Mount	S.	South	Yd.	Yard

District Abbreviations

D.L.   Dun Laoghaire

NOTES

The figures and letters following a street name indicate the postal district for that street with the square and page number where it will be found in the atlas. Thus the postal district for Abbey Park is 5 and it will be found in square O4 on page 25.

A street name followed by the name of another street in italics (not in brackets) does not appear on the map, but will be found adjoining or near the latter.

Abbey Cotts. 1	K 8 43	Albert Pl. 1	F 9 41	Annes La. 2	K 9 43
Abbey St. Upr.		*Inchicore Rd.*		Annesley Av. 3	M 7 36
Abbey Pk. 5	O 4 25	Albert Pl. W. 2	K10 43	Annesley Bridge 3	M 6 36
Abbey Pk., Baldoyle	U 2 28	Albert Rd., D.L.	W17 61	Annesley Bridge Rd. 3	M 6 36
Abbey Pk., D.L.	T17 60	Albert Ter. 2	K10 43	Annesley Pk. 6	L12 50
Abbey Rd., D.L.	T17 60	*Albert Pl. W.*		Annesley Pl. 3	M 7 36
Abbey St. Lwr. 1	K 8 43	Albert Vill. 4	M11 50	Appian Way, The, 6	L11 50
Abbey St. Mid. 1	K 8 43	*Morehampton Rd.*		Aranleigh Mount Av. 14	J16 55
Abbey St. Old. 1	L 8 44	Albion Ter. 8	F 9 41	Aranleigh Mount Ct. 14	J16 55
Abbey St. Upr.	K 8 43	*Inchicore Rd.*		Aranleigh Mount Pk. 14	J16 55
Abbey St., Howth	BB2 31	Aldborough Pl. 1	L 7 36	Aranleigh Mount Ter. 14	J16 55
Abbey Thea. 2	L 8 44	Alden Dr., Kilbarrack	T 3 28	Arbour Hill 7	H 8 42
Abbey View, D.L.	T17 60	Alden Pk., Kilbarrack	U 2 28	Arbour Pl. 7	H 8 42
Abbeyfield 5	P 4 26	Alden Rd., Kilbarrack	T 3 28	Arbour Ter. 7	H 8 42
Abbotstown Av. 11	E 3 20	Alders, The, D.L.	T16 60	Arbutus Av. 8	J11 49
Abbotstown Dr. 11	BB2 31	Aldrin Wk. 5	O 2 25	Arbutus Pl. 8	J10 43
Abbotstown Rd. 11	F 2 21	Alexandra Quay 1	O 8 45	Arcade 1	K 8 43
Abercorn Rd. 3	M 8 44	Alexandra Rd. 1	N 8 45	Ard Ri Pl. 7	H 8 42
Abercorn Ter. 7	H 7 34	Alexandra Ter. 3	Q 7 38	*Ard Ri Rd.*	
Abercorn Ter. 8	E 9 41	*Clontarf Rd.*		Ard Ri Rd. 7	H 8 42
Aberdeen St. 7	G 8 42	Alexandra Ter. 6	J13 49	Ardagh Rd. 12	G11 48
Achill Rd. 9	L 5 36	Alexandra Ter., Dundrum 14	M16 56	Ardbeg Cres. 5	P 3 26
Adam Ct. 2	K 9 43	All Hallows College 9	L 5 36	Ardbeg Dr. 5	P 3 26
Grafton St.		All Saints Dr. 5	R 4 27	Ardbeg Pk. 5	P 3 26
Adare Av. 5	O 2 25	All Saints Pk. 5	R 4 27	Ardbeg Rd. 5	P 3 26
Adare Dr. 5	P 2 26	All Saints Rd. 5	R 4 27	Ardcollum Av. 5	P 3 26
Adare Grn. 5	P 2 26	Allen Park Rd., Stillorgan	P16 58	Ardee Rd. 6	K11 49
Adare Pk. 5	P 2 26	Allen Pk., Stillorgan	P16 58	Ardee Row 8	J 9 43
Adare Rd. 5	P 2 26	Allingham St. 8	H 9 42	Ardee St. 8	J 9 43
Addison Pl. 9	K 5 35	Alma Rd., D.L.	S15 59	Ardenza Ter., D.L.	S15 59
Addison Rd. 3	M 6 36	Almeida Av. 8	G 9 42	Ardilaun Rd. 3	M 7 36
Addison Ter. 9	K 5 35	*Brookfield St.*		*Ballybough Rd.*	
Adelaide Conv. Home 14	K14 55	Almeida Ter. 8	G 9 42	Ardlea Rd. 5	O 3 25
Adelaide Rd. 2	K10 43	*Brookfield St.*		Ardmore Av. 7	H 7 34
Adelaide Rd., D.L.	W17 61	Altona Ter. 7	H 7 34	Ardmore Clo. 5	N 3 25
Adelaide St., D.L.	V16 61	Amiens St. 1	L 8 44	Ardmore Cres. 5	O 3 25
Adelaide Ter. 8	G 9 42	Anglesea Av., D.L.	R15 59	Ardmore Dr. 5	O 3 25
Brookfield St.		Anglesea Fruit Market 7	J 8 43	Ardmore Gro. 5	N 3 25
Adrian Av. 6	H12 48	*Green St. Lit.*		Ardmore Pk. 5	O 3 25
Aideen Av. 6	G13 48	Anglesea Market 1	K 8 43	Ardmore Pk., D.L.	T17 60
Aideen Dr. 6	H13 48	*Coles La.*		Ardpatrick Rd. 7	F 6 33
Aideen Pl. 6	H13 48	Anglesea Rd. 4	N12 51	Argyle Rd. 4	M11 50
Aifield Ct. 4	N13 51	Anglesea Row 7	K 8 43	Arklow St. 7	H 7 34
Aikenhead Ter. 4	N 9 45	Anglesea St. 2	K 9 43	Armagh Rd. 12	F12 47
Ailesbury Dr. 4	N12 51	Anna Villa 6	L12 50	Armstrong St. 6	J11 49
Ailesbury Gdns. 4	O12 51	Annadale Av. 3	M 6 36	*Harolds Cross Rd.*	
Ailesbury Gro. 4	N12 51	Annadale Cres. 9	M 5 36	Arnott St. 8	K10 43
Ailesbury Pk. 4	O12 51	Annadale Dr. 9	M 5 36	Arran Quay 7	J 8 43
Ailesbury Rd. 4	N12 51	Annaly Rd. 7	H 6 34	Arran Quay Ter. 7	J 8 43
Ainninn Av. 5	Q 3 26	Annamoe Dr. 7	H 7 34	Arran Rd. 9	L 5 36
Ainninn Dr. 5	Q 3 26	Annamoe Par. 7	H 7 34	Arran St. E. 7	J 8 43
Ainninn Pk. 5	Q 3 26	Annamoe Pk. 7	H 7 34	Arran St. W. 7	J 8 43
Airfield Pk. 4	N13 51	Annamoe Rd. 7	H 7 34	Arranmore Av. 7	K 6 35
Airfield Rd. 6	J13 49	Annamoe Ter. 7	H 7 34	Arranmore Rd. 4	M11 50
Albany Av., D.L.	T16 60	Annaville Gro. 14	M15 56	Arus An Uactarian 8	F 6 33
Albany Rd. 6	L12 50	Annaville Pk. 14	L15 56	Ascal An Charrain Chno 14	J16 55
Albert Agricultural College 9	L 3 24	Annaville Ter. 14	M15 56	*(Nutgrove Av.)*	
Albert Av. 5	K 3 23	*Annaville Gro.*		Ascal Bhaile An Abba 11	F 3 21
Albert College Cres. 9	K 3 23	Anne Devlin Av. 14	G16 54	*(Abbotstown Av.)*	
Albert College Dr. 9	K 3 23	Anne Devlin Dr. 14	G16 54	Ascal Mac Amhlaoi 5	Q 3 26
Albert College Lawn 9	K 3 23	Anne Devlin Pk. 14	G16 54	*(McAuley Av.)*	
Albert College Pk. 9	K 3 23	Anne Devlin Rd. 14	G16 54	Ascal Measc 5	P 3 26
Albert College Ter. 9	K 3 23	Anne St. N. 7	J 8 43	*(Mask Av.)*	
Albert, D.L.	W17 61	Anne St. S. 2	K 9 43	Ascal Ratabhachta 11	BB3 31
Albert Pl. 2	M 9 44	Anner Rd. 8	F 9 41	*(Rathoath Av.)*	

Name	Ref
Asgard Pk., Howth	BB3 31
Asgard Rd., Howth	BB3 31
Ash St. 8	J 9 43
Ashbrook, Castleknock	D 5 32
Ashcroft 5	R 3 27
Ashdale Av. 6	H13 48
Ashdale Gdns. 6	H13 48
Ashdale Pk. 6	H13 48
Ashdale Rd. 6	H13 48
Ashfield Av. 6	L12 50
Ashfield Clo. 6	F15 53
Ashfield Rd.	
Ashfield Pk. 6	F15 53
Ashfield Rd.	
Ashfield Pk. 6	H13 48
Ashfield Pk., Booterstown	O14 57
Ashfield Rd. 6	F15 53
Ashfield Rd. 6	L12 50
Ashford Cotts. 7	H 7 34
Ashford St.	
Ashford Pl. 7	H 7 34
Ashford St.	
Ashford St. 7	H 7 34
Ashgrove, D.L.	T17 60
Ashington Av. 7	F 5 33
Ashington Pk. 7	E 5 33
Ashington Ri. 7	E 5 33
Ashton Pk., D.L.	T16 60
Ashtown Gro. 7	E 5 33
Ashtown Rd., Castleknock	D 5 32
Ashtown Station	AA4 31
Aston Pl. 2	K 8 43
Aston Quay 2	K 8 43
Athlumney Vill. 6	K11 49
Auburn Av. 4	M12 50
Auburn Rd. 4	M12 50
Auburn Av.	
Auburn St. 7	J 7 35
Auburn Vill. 6	J13 49
Audilaun Rd. 3	L 7 36
Aughavanagh Rd. 12	H11 48
Aughrim La. 7	H 7 34
Aughrim Pl. 7	H 7 34
Aughrim St. 7	H 7 34
Aughrim Vill. 7	H 7 34
Aughrim St.	
Aungier Pl. 2	K 9 43
Aungier St. 2	K 9 43
Ave Maria Rd. 8	H10 42
Avenue Rd. 8	J11 49
Bloomfield Av.	
Avoca Av., D.L.	Q15 58
Avoca Pl., D.L.	R15 59
Avoca Rd., D.L.	Q16 58
Avondale Av. 7	J 7 35
Avondale Lawn Ext., D.L.	R16 59
Avondale Lawn, D.L.	R16 59
Avondale Pk. 5	S 4 27
Avondale Rd. 7	J 7 35
Ayrefield Av. 5	Q 2 26
Ayrefield Ct. 5	Q 2 26
Ayrefield Dr. 5	Q 2 26
Ayrefield Gro. 5	Q 2 26
Ayrefield Pk. 5	Q 2 26
Bachelors Wk. 1	K 8 43
Back La. 8	J 9 43
Back La., Baldoyle	V 1 EE
Baggot Ct. 2	
Baggot La. 4	M10 44
Baggot Rd. 7	E 6 33
Baggot St. Lwr. 2	L10 44
Baggot St. Upr. 4	M10 44
Baggot Ter. 7	E 6 33
Blackhorse Av.	
Bailey Green Rd., Howth	BB4 31
Baldoyle Rd.	W 2 29
Balfe Av. 12	E12 47
Balfe Rd. 12	E12 47
Balfe Rd. E. 12	E12 47
Balfe St. 2	K 9 43
Harry St.	
Balfe St. 2	K 9 43
Chatham St.	
Balglass Rd., Howth	BB3 31
Balkill Pk., Howth	AA3 31
Balkill Rd., Howth	BB3 31
Ballsbridge Av. 4	N11 51
Ballsbridge Ter. 4	N11 51
Ballsbridge	
Ballyboggan Rd. 11	F 4 21
Ballybough Av. 3	M 7 36
Spring Garden St.	
Ballybough Cotts. 3	M 6 36
Ballybough Ct. 3	M 6 36
Ballybough St. 3	M 7 36
Spring Garden St.	
Ballybough Rd. 3	M 7 36
Ballyfermot Av. 10	C 9 40
Ballyfermot Cres. 10	C 9 40
Ballyfermot Hill 10	C 8 40
Ballyfermot Par. 10	C 9 40
Ballygall Av. 11	H 2 22
Ballygall Cres. 11	G 3 22
Ballygall Par. 11	G 3 22
Ballygall Pl. 11	H 3 22
Ballygall Rd. E. 11	J 3 23
Ballygall Rd. W. 11	G 3 22
Ballygihen Av., D.L.	W17 61
Ballyhoy Av. 5	R 4 27
(Ascal Bhaile Thuaidh)	
Ballyhoy Av. 5	R 4 27
Ballymace Grn. 14	F16 53
Ballymount Dr. 12	C13 46
Ballyneety Rd. 10	D 9 40
Ballyroan Cres. 14	G16 54
Ballyroan Heights 14	G16 54
Ballyroan Pk. 14	F16 53
Ballyroan Rd. 14	F16 53
Ballyshannon Av. 5	N 2 25
Ballyshannon Rd. 5	N 2 25
Ballytore Rd. 14	J14 55
Balscadden Rd., Howth	BB3 31
Bancroft Clo., Tallaght	C16 52
Bancroft Gro., Tallaght	C16 52
Bancroft Rd., Tallaght	C16 52
Bangor Dr. 12	G11 48
Bangor Rd. 12	G11 48
Bank of Ireland 2	K 9 43
Bankside Cotts. 14	L14 56
Bann Rd. 11	G 5 34
Bannow Rd. 7	G 5 34
Bantry Rd. 9	K 4 23
Barclay Ct., D.L.	R15 59
Bargy Rd. 3	N 7 37
Barnamore Cres. 11	G 4 22
Barnamore Gro.	
Barnamore Gro. 11	G 4 22
Barnamore Pk. 11	G 4 22
Barrack St. 11	G 3 22
Barrett St. 11	U16 60
Barrow Rd. 11	H 5 34
Barrow St. 4	M 9 44
Barry Av. 11	F 2 21
Barry Dr. 11	F 2 21
Barry Grn. 11	F 2 21
Barry Pk. 11	F 2 21
Barry Rd. 11	F 2 21
Barryscourt Rd. 5	O 2 25
Barton Dr. 14	H16 54
Basin St. Lwr. 8	H 9 42
Basin St. Upr. 8	H 9 42
Basin View Ter. 7	K 7 35
Bass Pl. 2	L 9 44
Bath Av. 4	N10 45
Bath Avenue Gdns. 4	N10 45
Bath Avenue Pl. 4	N10 45
Bath La. 1	K 7 35
Bath Pl., D.L.	R15 59
Bath St. 4	N 9 45
Baymount Pk. 3	R 6 39
Bayside Boulevard N., Kilbarrack	U 2 28
Bayside Cres., Kilbarrack	U 2 28
Bayside Pk., Kilbarrack	U 2 28
Bayside Sq. E., Kilbarrack	U 2 28
Bayside Sq. N., Kilbarrack	V 3 29
Bayside Sq. S., Kilbarrack	U 3 28
Bayside Wk., Kilbarrack	U 2 28
Bayview 4	N 9 45
Pembroke St.	
Bayview Av. 3	M 7 36
Beach Av. 4	O10 45
Beach Dr. 4	O10 45
Beach Rd. 4	O10 45
Beattys Av. 4	N11 51
Beaufield Pk., Stillorgan	P16 58
Beaufort Downs 14	H16 54
Beaumont Av. 14	L16 56
Beaumont Clo. 14	K16 55
Beaumont Cres. 9	N 3 25
Beaumont Dr. 14	L16 56
Beaumont Gro. 9	M 3 24
Beaumont Rd. 9	M 4 24
Beauvale Pk. 5	O 3 25
Beaver Row 4	M13 50
Beaver St. 1	L 8 44
Bedford Row 2	K 9 43
Temple Bar	
Beech Gro., D.L.	Q14 58
Beech Hill Av. 4	N13 51
Beech Hill Cres. 4	N13 51
Beech Hill Dr. 4	N13 51
Beech Hill Ter. 4	N13 51
Beech Hill Vill. 4	N13 51
Beech Hill Ter.	
Beech Park Av. 5	P 2 26
Beeches, The 5	S 2 27
Beechfield Av. 12	E13 47
Beechfield Clo. 12	E13 47
Beechfield Rd. 12	E13 47
Beechmount Dr. 14	M14 56
Beechwood Av. Lwr. 6	L12 50
Beechwood Av. Upr. 6	L12 50
Beechwood Pk. 6	K12 49
Beechwood Pk., D.L.	V17 61
Beechwood Rd. 6	L12 50
Beggarsbush Barracks 4	M10 44
Belfield Downs 4	M15 56
Belgrave Av. 6	K12 49
Belgrave Pl. 6	K12 49
Belgrave Rd. 6	K12 49
Belgrave Rd., D.L.	S15 59
Belgrave Sq. E. 6	K12 49
Belgrave Sq. E., D.L.	T15 60
Belgrave Sq. N. 6	K12 49
Belgrave Sq. N., D.L.	S15 59
Belgrave Sq. S. 6	K12 49
Belgrave Sq. S., D.L.	S15 59
Belgrave Sq. W. 6	K12 49
Belgrave Sq. W., D.L.	S15 59
Belgrave Ter., D.L.	S15 59
Belgrove Lawn, Chapelizod	C 8 40
Belgrove Pk., Chapelizod	C 8 40
Belgrove Rd. 3	P 7 38
Bella St. 1	L 7 36
Belle Bank 8	H 9 42
Belleville Av. 6	J13 49
Bellevue 8	H 9 42
Bellevue Av. 4	P13 63
Bellevue Pk., Stillorgan	P13 63
Belmont Av. 4	M12 50
Belmont Ct. 4	M12 50
Belmont Av.	
Belmont Gdns. 4	M12 50
Belmont Pk. 4	M12 50
Belmont Vill. 4	M12 50
Belton Park Av. 9	N 4 25
Belton Park Gdns. 9	N 4 25
Belton Park Rd. 9	N 4 25
Belton Park Vill. 9	N 5 37
Belvidere Av. 1	L 7 36
Belvidere Ct. 1	K 7 35
Belvidere Pl. 1	K 7 35
Belvidere Rd. 1	K 7 35
Belview Bldgs. 8	H 9 42
School St.	
Ben Edar Rd. 7	H 7 34
Ben Inagh Pk., Booterstown	R14 59
Benbulbin Av. 12	F11 47
Benbulbin Rd. 12	F10 41
Benburb St. 7	H 8 42
Beneavin Dr. 11	J 3 23
Beneavin Pk. 11	H 2 22
Beneavin Rd. 11	H 2 22
Bengal Ter. 9	J 5 35
Benmadigan Rd. 12	F10 41
Benson St. 2	N 9 45
Beresford La. 1	L 8 44
Beresford Pl. 1	L 8 44
Beresford St. 7	J 8 43
Berkeley Rd. 7	K 7 35
Berkeley St. 7	K 7 35
Berryfield Cres. 11	F 3 21
Berryfield Rd.	
Berryfield Ct. 11	F 3 21
Berryfield Dr. 11	F 3 21
Berryfield Rd. 11	F 3 21
Bessborough Av. 3	M 7 36
Bessborough Par. 6	K11 49
Bethesda Pl. 1	K 7 35
Dorset St. Upr.	
Bettyglen 5	T 4 28
Bettystown Av. 5	R 4 27
Big Bridge	H14 54
Bigger Rd. 12	E12 47
Binn Eadair Vw., Sutton	W 2 29
Binns Bridge	K 6 35
Birchfield 14	N16 57
Birchgrove, D.L.	T17 60
Birchs La. 14	M16 56
Bird Av. 14	M14 56
Bishop St. 8	K10 43
Black Pitts 8	J10 43
Black St. 7	G 8 42
Blackberry La. 6	K11 49
Blackhall Par. 7	J 8 43
Blackhall Pl. 7	H 8 42
Blackhall St. 7	J 8 43
Blackheath Av. 3	Q 6 38
Blackheath Dr. 3	P 6 38
Blackheath Gdns. 3	P 6 38
Blackheath Gro. 3	P 6 38
Blackheath Pk. 3	P 6 38
Blackhorse Av. 7	D 5 32
Blackhorse Bridge	E10 41
Blackhorse Gro. 7	H 7 34
Blackrock College	Q14 58
Blackrock Station	R14 59
Blackwater Rd. 11	H 5 34
Blarney Pk. 12	G12 48
Blessington Ct. 7	K 7 35
Blessington St.	
Blessington St. 7	K 7 35
Bloomfield Av., Portobello 8	J10 43

Name	Grid
Bloomfield Av., Donnybrook 4	L11 50
Bloomfield Pk. 8	J11 49
Bluebell Av. 12	D11 46
Bluebell Rd. 12	D11 46
Blythe Av. 3	M8 43
Church Rd.	
Boden Wood 14	H16 54
Bolton St. 1	K8 43
Bon Secours Hospital 9	K4 23
Bond Rd. 3	N8 45
Bond St. 8	H9 42
Bonham St. 8	H9 42
Boolavogue Rd. 3	M7 36
Booterstown Av., D.L.	P15 58
Booterstown Pk., D.L.	P15 58
Botanic Av. 9	K5 35
Botanic Gdns.	J5 35
Botanic Pk. 9	K5 35
Botanic Rd. 9	Q4 26
Botanic Vill. 9	J6 35
Botanic Rd.	K5 35
Bothar Chille Na Manac 12	D12 46
(Walkinstown Rd.)	
Bothar Coilbeard 8	F9 41
Bow Bridge 8	G9 42
Bow La. E. 2	K9 43
Bow La. W. 8	G9 42
Bow St. 7	J8 43
Boyne La. 2	L9 44
Boyne Rd. 11	G5 34
Boyne St. 2	L9 44
Br. Ainninn 5	Q3 26
(Ennel Rd.)	
Br. Aird An Tobair 11	F4 21
(Springmount Rd.)	
Br. An Easa 5	R4 27
(Watermill Rd.)	
Br. Dhroichead Ciardiubh 11	F3 21
(Cardiffsbridge Rd.)	
Br. Phairc An Bhailtini 7	F6 33
(Villa Park Rd.)	
Br. Raitleann 12	G13 48
(Rathland Rd.)	
Brabazon Row 8	J10 43
Brabazon Sq. 8	J9 43
Pimlico	
Brabazon St. 8	J9 43
Brackens La. 2	L8 44
Braemor Av. 14	K15 55
Braemor Dr. 14	K15 55
Braemor Gro. 14	K15 55
Braemor Pk. 14	K14 55
Braemor Rd. 14	K15 55
Bramborough Ter. 8	H10 42
South Circular Rd.	
Braithwaite St. 8	H9 42
Brakens La. 2	L8 44
Moss St.	
Branch Rd. S. 1	P8 62
Brandon Rd. 12	E11 47
Bregia Rd. 7	H6 34
Brehan Rd. 4	O9 45
Bremen Av. 4	O10 45
Bremen Gro. 4	O10 45
Brendan Dr. 5	P3 26
(Ceide Brendain)	
Brendon Rd. 4	M11 50
Brian Av. 3	M5 36
Brian Boru Av. 3	Q7 38
Brian Boru St. 3	Q7 38
Brian Rd. 3	M6 36
Brian Ter. 3	M6 36
Briarfield Gro. 5	T3 28
Briarfield Rd. 5	S3 27
Briarfield Vill. 5	T3 28
Brickfield Dr. 12	G10 42
Brickfield La. 8	H10 42
Bride Rd. 8	J9 43
Bride St. 8	J9 43
Bride St. New 8	K10 43
Bridge St. 4	N9 45
Bridge St. Lwr. 8	J9 43
Bridge St. Upr. 8	J9 43
Bridgefoot St. 8	J9 43
Brighton Av. 3	N6 37
Brighton Av. 6	J13 49
Brighton Av., D.L.	T16 60
Brighton Gdns. 6	J13 49
Brighton Rd. 6	J13 49
Brighton Sq. 6	J13 49
Brighton Vale, D.L.	S15 59
Britain Pl. 1	K8 43
Britain Quay 2	N9 45
Broadstone 7	J7 35
Broadstone Av. 7	J7 35
Phibsborough Rd.	
Brook Ct., D.L.	T16 60
Brookfield 5	Q3 26
Brookfield 6	L13 50
Brookfield Av., D.L.	R15 59
Brookfield Pl., D.L.	R15 59

Name	Grid
Brookfield Rd. 8	G9 42
Brookfield St. 8	G9 42
Brookfield, D.L.	Q15 58
Brooklands 4	O12 51
Brooklawn 3	O6 37
Brooklawn, D.L.	Q15 58
Brookvale Downs 14	H14 54
Brookvale Rd. 4	M12 50
Brookville Cres. 5	P2 26
Brookville Pk. 5	Q2 26
Brookwood Av. 5	P4 26
Brookwood Cres. 5	Q4 26
Brookwood Dr. 5	P4 26
Brookwood Gro. 5	P4 26
Brookwood Heights 5	P4 26
Brookwood Lawn 5	Q4 26
Brookwood Meadow 5	P4 26
Brookwood Pk. 5	P4 26
Brookwood Rd. 5	P4 26
Brookwood Rise 5	Q4 26
Broombridge Rd. 7	G5 34
Brown St. N. 7	J8 43
Brown St. S. 8	H10 42
Brunswick Pl. 2	M9 44
Pearse St.	
Brunswick St. N. 7	J8 43
Buckingham St. Lwr. 1	L7 36
Buckingham St. Upr. 1	L7 36
Bulfin Gdns. 8	F9 41
Bulfin Rd. 8	F10 41
Bulfin St. 8	F9 41
Bull Alley St. 8	J9 43
Bunratty Av. 5	P2 26
Bunratty Dr. 5	P2 26
Bunratty Rd. 5	O2 25
Bunting Rd. 12	D12 46
Burdett Av., D.L.	W17 61
Burgess La. 7	J8 43
Haymarket	
Burgh Quay 2	K8 43
Burke Pl. 8	G9 42
Burlington Rd. 4	L10 44
Burris Ct. 8	J9 43
School House La. W.	
Burrowfield Rd., Baldoyle	W2 29
Bushfield Av. 4	M12 50
Bushfield Ter. 4	L12 50
Bushy Park Gdns. 6	J14 55
Bushy Park Rd. 6	H14 54
Butterfield Av. 14	F16 53
Butterfield Cl. 14	G16 54
Butterfield Cres. 14	H15 54
Butterfield Gro. 14	H16 54
Butterfield Orchard 14	H16 54
Butterfield Pk. 14	G16 54
Byrnes La. 1	K8 43
Cabra Dr. 7	H6 34
Cabra Gro. 7	H6 34
Cabra Pk. 7	J6 35
Cabra Rd. 7	G6 34
Cadogan Rd. 3	M6 36
Calderwood Av. 9	M4 24
Calderwood Clo. 9	M5 36
Calderwood Gro. 9	M5 36
Calderwood Rd. 9	M5 36
Caledon Rd. 3	M7 36
Callary Rd.,Stillorgan	O15 57
Camac Pk. 12	C11 46
Camac Ter. 8	G9 42
Bow Bridge	
Cambells Ct. 7	J8 43
Little Britain St.	
Cambridge Av. 4	O9 45
Cambridge La. 6	K12 49
Cambridge Rd. 4	N9 45
Cambridge Rd., Rathmines 6	K12 49
Cambridge St. 4	N9 45
Cambridge Ter. 6	L11 50
Cambridge Vill. 6	K12 49
Belgrave Rd.	
Camden Market 2	K10 43
Camden St. Lwr.	
Camden Pl. 2	K10 43
Camden Row 8	K10 43
Camden St. Lwr. 2	K10 43
Camden St. Upr. 2	K10 43
Cameron Sq. 8	F10 41
Connolly Av.	
Cameron Sq. 8	G9 42
Cameron St. 8	H10 42
Campbells Row 1	L7 36
Portland St. N.	
Canal Bank 8	E10 41
Goldenbridge	
Canal Rd. 6	K11 49
Canal Ter. 12	D10 40
Canning Pl. 1	M8 44
Cannon Rock Vw., Howth	BB3 31
Canon Lillis Av. 1	M8 44
Capel St. 1	K8 43
Cappagh Av. 11	F2 21

Name	Grid
Cappagh Dr. 11	F3 21
Cappagh Rd. 11	E2 21
Captains Av. 12	F12 47
Captains Dr. 12	F12 47
Captains Rd. 12	F12 47
Caragh Rd. 7	G7 34
Carberry Rd. 9	M5 36
Cardiff Bridge	J7 35
Phibsborough Rd.	
Cardiff Castle Rd. 11	F3 21
Cardiffs La. 2	M9 44
Cardiffsbridge Av. 11	F3 21
Cardiffsbridge Rd. 11	F3 21
Cards La. 2	L9 44
Townsend St.	
Carleton Rd. 3	N6 37
Carlingford Par. 2	M9 44
Carlingford Rd. 9	K6 35
Carlisle Av. 4	M12 50
Carlisle St. 8	J10 43
Carmans Hall 8	J9 43
Carndonagh Dr. 5	T2 28
Carndonagh Lawn 5	T2 28
Carndonagh Pk. 5	T2 28
Carndonagh Rd. 5	T2 28
Carnew St. 7	H7 34
Carnlough Rd. 7	G5 34
Caroline Row 4	N9 45
Bridge St.	
Carraroe Av. 5	S2 27
Carrick Brennan Lawn, D.L.	T16 60
Carrick Ter. 8	H10 42
Carrickbrack Heath, Howth	Y3 30
Carrickbrack Hill, Howth	Y3 30
Carrickbrack Lawn, Howth	Y4 30
Carrickbrack Rd., Howth	Y4 30
Carrickbrennan Rd., D.L.	T16 60
Carrickmount Av. 14	K16 55
Carrickmount Dr. 14	K16 55
Carrickmount Pk. 14	K16 55
Carrigallen Dr. 11	G4 22
Carrigallen Rd.	
Carrigallen Pk. 11	G4 22
Carrigallen Rd.	
Carrigallen Rd. 11	G4 22
Carrow Rd. 12	E10 41
Carysfort Av., D.L.	R16 59
Casana Vw., Howth	BB4 31
Casement Dr. 11	F2 21
Casement Grn. 11	F2 21
Casement Gro. 11	F2 21
Casement Pk. 11	F2 21
Casement Pk., D.L.	T17 60
Casement Rd. 11	G3 22
Cashel Av. 12	G13 48
Cashel Rd. 12	F11 47
Casimir Av. 6	J12 49
Casimir Rd. 6	H12 48
Casino Rd. 3	M5 36
Castilla Pk. 3	Q6 38
Castle Av. 3	P6 38
Castle Ct. 3	O6 37
Howth Rd.	
Castle Ct., D.L.	O6 37
Castle Ct., D.L.	P14 58
Castle Golf Course	J15 55
Castle Gro. 3	P5 38
Castle Lawns, Tallaght	C16 52
Castle Market 2	K9 43
Drury St.	
Castle Pk., D.L.	T16 60
Castle Rd. 3	P6 38
Castle St. 2	K9 43
Castlebyrne Pk., Stillorgan	R16 59
Castleforbes Rd. 1	N8 45
Castlekevin Rd. 5	O2 25
Castlepark Rd., D.L.	W17 61
Castleside Dr. 14	J15 55
Castletimon Av. 5	N2 25
Castletimon Dr. 5	N2 25
Castletimon Gdns. 9	N2 25
Castletimon Grn. 5	N2 25
Castletimon Pk. 5	N2 25
Castletimon Rd. 5	N2 25
Castlewood Av. 6	K12 49
Castlewood Clo. 6	K12 49
Castlewood Av.	
Castlewood La. 6	K12 49
Castlewood Pk. 6	K12 49
Castlewood Pl. 6	K12 49
Castlewood Ter. 6	K12 49
Cathal Brugha St. 1	K8 43
Cathedral La. 8	J10 43
Cathedral St. 1	K8 43
Catherine St. 8	H9 42
Thomas St.	
Catherines La. 7	J8 43
Church St. Old	
Cavendish Row 1	K8 43
Parnell St.	
Ceannt Fort 8	G9 42
Cecil Av. 3	N6 37

Name	Grid
Cecilia St. 2	K 9 43
Temple La. S.	
Cedar Ct. 6	H13 48
Cedar Pk. 5	S 2 27
Cedar Wk. 5	S 3 27
Cedarmount Rd., Stillorgan	O10 57
Cedars, The, D.L.	T16 60
Cedarwood Av. 11	H 2 22
Cedarwood Clo. 11	J 2 23
Cedarwood Grn. 11	H 2 22
Cedarwood Gro. 11	H 2 22
Cedarwood Pk. 11	H 2 22
Cedarwood Ri. 11	H 2 22
Ceide Bhaile An Dein 11	F 3 21
Faithche Bhaile An Dein	
Ceide Brendain 5	P 3 26
(Brendan Dr.)	
Ceide Gleannaluinn, Chapelizod	C 8 40
(Glenaulin Dr.)	
Ceide Phairc An Bhailtini 7	F 6 33
(Villa Park Dr.)	
Celestine Av. 4	N 9 45
Celtic Park Av. 9	N 4 25
Celtic Park Rd. 9	N 4 25
Central Mental Hospital 14	M15 56
Chamber St. 8	J10 43
Chancery La. 8	K 9 43
Chancery Pl. 7	J 8 43
Chancery St. 7	J 8 43
Chanel Av. 5	P 3 26
Chanel Gro. 5	P 2 26
Chanel Rd. 5	P 3 26
Chapel Av. 4	N 9 45
Chapel La. 1	K 8 43
Chapelizod Ct. 10	C 8 40
Chapelizod Hill Rd. 10	C 8 40
Chapelizod Rd. 8	D 8 40
Charlemont Av., D.L.	V16 61
Charlemont Bridge	K11 49
Charlemont Gdns. 2	K10 43
Charlemont St.	
Charlemont Mall 2	K11 49
Charlemont Par. 3	M 7 36
Charlemont Pl. 2	K11 49
Charlemont Rd. 3	N 6 37
Charlemont Sq. 2	K10 43
Charlemont St.	
Charlemont St. 2	K10 43
Charles La. Gt. 1	L 7 36
Charles St. 1	L 7 36
Charles St. W. 7	J 8 43
Charleston Av. 6	K12 49
Charleston Rd. 6	L11 50
Charleville 14	L15 56
Charleville Av. 3	M 7 36
Charleville Mall 1	L 7 36
Charleville Rd. 6	J12 49
Charleville Rd. 7	H 7 34
Charlotte Quay 4	M 9 44
Charlotte St. 2	K10 43
Chatham Row 2	K 9 43
William St. S.	
Chatham St. 2	K 9 43
Chaworth Ter. 8	J 9 43
Hanbury La	
Cheaters La. 2	K10 43
Redmonds Hill	
Chelmsford Rd. 6	L11 50
Chelsea Gdns. 3	Q 6 38
Cheltenham Pl. 6	K11 49
Portobello Bridge	
Cherbury Ct., D.L.	P15 58
Cherbury Gdns., D.L.	P15 58
Cherry Garth, Stillorgan	P16 58
Chieffy Gro. 12	E13 47
Cherryfield Av., Walkinstown 12	E13 47
Cherryfield Av., Ranelagh 6	L12 50
Cherryfield Dr. 12	E13 47
Cherryfield Rd. 12	E13 47
Cherrymount Cres. 9	N 5 37
Cherrymount Pk. 7	J 7 35
Chester Rd. 6	L11 50
Chestnut Rd., Stillorgan	O15 57
Christ Church Cathedral 8	J 9 43
Christchurch Pl. 8	J 9 43
Church Av. N., Drumcondra 9	L 5 36
Church Av., Glasnevin 9	K 4 23
Church Av., Irishtown 4	O10 45
Church Av., Rathmines 6	K12 49
Church Av., Rialto 8	G10 42
Church Gdns. 6	K12 49
Church La. S. 8	K 9 43
College Grn	
Church La. S. 8	K10 43
Kevin St. Lwr.	
Church La., Rathfarnham 14	H15 54
Church Rd. 3	M 8 44
Church Rd., Finglas 11	G 3 22
Church St. E. 3	M 8 44
Church St. New 7	J 8 43
Church St. Upr. 7	J 8 43
Church St., Finglas 11	G 3 22
Churchgate Av. 3	Q 7 38
Churchill Ter. 4	N11 51
Churchtown Av. 14	L14 56
Churchtown Clo. 14	L14 56
Churchtown Dr. 14	L14 56
Churchtown Rd. 14	K15 55
Churchtown Rd. Upr. 14	L16 56
Cian Pk. 9	L 6 36
Cill Eanna 5	Q 4 26
City Quay 2	L 8 44
Civic Guards Depot 8	G 7 34
Clanawley Rd. 5	P 5 38
Clanboy Rd. 5	O 4 25
Clanbrassil St. Lwr. 8	J10 43
Clanbrassil St. Upr. 8	J11 49
Clancy Av. 11	G 2 22
Clancy Barracks 8	G 8 42
Clancy Rd. 11	H 2 22
Clandonagh Rd. 5	O 4 25
Clanhugh Rd. 5	O 5 37
Clanmahon Rd. 5	P 5 38
Clanmaurice Rd. 5	O 4 25
Clanmoyle Rd. 5	O 5 37
Clanranald Rd. 5	O 5 37
Clanree Rd. 5	O 4 25
Clanwilliam Pl. 2	M10 44
Clare La. 2	L 9 44
Clare Rd. 9	L 5 36
Clare St. 2	L 9 44
Claremont Av. 9	K 4 23
Claremont Ct. 11	H 5 34
Claremont Dr. 11	J 3 23
Claremont Pk. 4	O10 45
(Pairc Clearmont)	
Claremont Rd. 4	O10 45
Claremont Vill., D.L.	V17 61
Clarence Mangan Rd. 8	J10 43
Clarence St. Gt. N. 1	L 7 36
Clarence St., D.L.	U15 60
Clarendon Market 2	K 9 43
Chatham St.	
Clarendon Row 2	K 9 43
Clarendon St.	
Clarendon St. 2	K 9 43
Clareville Ct. 11	J 5 35
Clareville Gro. 11	J 5 35
Clareville Pk. 11	J 5 35
Clareville Rd. 6	H12 48
Clarinda Pk. E., D.L.	V17 61
Clarinda Pk. N., D.L.	V16 61
Clarinda Pk. W., D.L.	V17 61
Classons Bridge	L14 56
Claude Rd. 9	K 6 35
Clifton Av., D.L.	T16 60
Clifton Ter., D.L.	T16 60
Cliftonville Rd. 9	K 5 35
Clinches Ct. 3	M 7 36
Clogher Rd. 12	G11 48
Cloisters, The 6	H13 48
Clonard Rd. 12	G12 48
Clonfert Rd. 12	G12 48
Clonlara Rd. 4	O 9 45
Clonliffe Av. 3	L 6 36
Clonliffe Gdns. 3	L 6 36
Clonliffe Rd. 3	L 6 36
Clonmacnoise Rd. 12	G12 48
Clonmel Rd. 11	J 3 23
Clonmore Rd., Ballybough 3	L 7 36
Clonmore Rd., Stillorgan	O16 57
Clonmore Ter. 3	L 7 36
Clonrosse Ct. 5	R 2 27
Elton Dr.	
Clonrosse Dr. 5	R 2 27
Clonrosse Pk. 5	R 2 27
Elton Dr.	
Clonshaugh Rd. 5	O 2 25
Clonskeagh Bridge	M13 50
Clonskeagh Castle 14	L13 50
Clonskeagh Rd. 14	M12 50
Clontarf Castle 3	P 6 38
Clontarf Golf Course 3	O 5 37
Clontarf Pk. 3	Q 7 38
Clontarf Promenade 3	O 7 37
Clontarf Rd. 3	N 6 37
Clontarf Station	O 6 37
Clonturk Av. 9	L 5 36
Clonturk Gdns. 9	L 5 36
Clonturk Pk. 9	L 5 36
Cloonlara Cres. 11	G 4 22
Cloonlara Rd.	
Cloonlara Dr. 11	G 4 22
Cloonlara Rd.	
Cloonlara Rd. 11	G 4 22
Close, The, Stillorgan	P15 58
Cloyne Rd. 12	G12 48
Club Rd., Walkinstown	C12 46
Clune Rd. 11	G 2 22
Clyde La. 4	M11 50
Clyde Rd. 4	M11 50
Coburg Pl. 1	M 8 44
Coldwell St., D.L.	V17 61
Colepark Av. 10	C 9 40
Colepark Dr. 10	C 9 40
Coleraine St. 7	J 8 43
College Cres. 6	F14 53
College Dr. 6	G14 54
College Grn. 2	K 9 43
College La. 2	L 9 44
Westland Row	
College Pk. 6	F14 53
College St. 2	K 9 43
Colliers Av. 6	L12 50
Collins Av. 9	M 4 24
Collins Av. E. 5	O 4 25
Collins Av. Ext. 9	K 3 23
Collins Av. W. 9	L 3 24
Collins Barracks 7	H 8 42
Collins Dr. 11	H 2 22
Collins Grn. 11	H 2 22
Collins Pk. 9	N 4 25
Collins Pl. 11	H 3 22
Collins Row 11	H 3 22
Comeragh Rd. 12	E11 47
Commons St. 1	L 8 44
Congress Gdns., D.L.	W17 61
Connaught St. 7	J 6 35
Connaught Ter. 6	J13 49
Rathgar Rd.	
Connolly Av. 8	F 9 41
Connolly Station 1	L 8 44
Conor Clune Rd. 7	E 6 33
Conquer Hill Rd. 3	Q 7 38
Conquer Hill Ter. 3	Q 6 38
Constitution Hill 7	J 8 43
Convent Av. 3	M 6 36
Convent La. 14	H16 54
Convent Rd., D.L.	R15 59
Convent Rd., D.L.	U16 60
Convent View Cotts. 7	F 5 33
Conyngham Rd. 8	F 8 41
Cook St. 8	J 9 43
Cooks La. 3	H 9 42
Coolamber Pk. 14	F16 53
Coolatree Pk. 9	M 3 24
Coolatree Rd. 9	N 3 25
Cooleen Av. 9	M 2 24
Cooley Rd. 12	E10 41
Coolgariff Rd. 9	M 3 24
Coolgreena Clo. 9	N 3 25
Coolgreena Rd. 9	N 3 25
Coolock Av. 5	P 2 26
Coolock Clo. 5	P 2 26
Coolock Ct. 5	P 2 26
Coolock Dr. 5	P 2 26
Coolock Grn. 5	P 2 26
Coolock Gro. 5	P 3 26
Coolock Village 5	P 3 26
Coolrua Dr. 9	M 3 24
Coombe, The, 8	J 9 43
Cope St. 2	K 9 43
Copeland Av. 3	N 6 37
Copeland Gro. 3	N 6 37
Copper Alley 8	K 9 43
Coppingers Row 2	K 9 43
William St. S.	
Corballis Row 8	J10 43
Kevin St. Upr.	
Cork Hill 2	K 9 43
Cork St. 8	H10 42
Cormack Ter. 6	H14 54
Corn Exchange Pl. 2	L 8 44
George's Quay	
Cornmarket 8	J 9 43
Corporation Bldgs. 8	G 9 42
Corporation Pl. 1	L 8 44
Corporation St. 1	L 8 44
Corrib Rd. 6	G13 48
CorrigAv., D.L.	V17 61
Corrig Castle Ter., D.L.	V16 61
Corrig Clo. 12	C14 52
Lugnaquilla Av.	
Corrig Pk., D.L.	V17 61
Corrig Rd., D.L.	V17 61
Cottage Pl. 1	K 6 35
Portland Pl.	
Coulson Av. 6	J13 49
Coultry Way 9	L 2 24
Courts of Justice 7	J 8 43
Cow Parlour 8	J10 43
Cowbooter La., Howth	BB3 31
Cowley Pl. 7	K 6 35
Cowper Downs 6	K13 49
Cowper Dr. 6	L13 50
Cowper Gdns. 6	L13 50
Cowper Rd. 6	K13 49
Cowper St. 7	H 7 34
Craigford Av. 5	O 4 25
Craigford Dr. 5	O 4 25
Craigmore Gdns., D.L.	S15 59
Crampton Bldgs. 2	K 9 43
Temple Bar	
Crampton Ct. 2	K 9 43
Crampton Quay 2	K 8 43

Name	Grid
Crane La. 2	K 9 43
Crane St. 8	H 9 42
Cranfield Pl. 4	O10 45
Cranford Ct. 4	O13 51
Cranmer La. 4	M10 44
Crannagh Gro. 14	J14 55
Crannagh Pk. 14	J15 55
Crannagh Rd. 14	H15 54
Crawford Av. 9	K 6 35
Creighton St. 2	L 9 44
Cremona Rd. 10	C 9 40
Cremore Av. 11	J 4 23
Cremore Cres. 11	J 4 23
Cremore Dr. 11	J 4 23
Cremore Lawn 11	J 4 23
Cremore Pk. 11	J 4 23
Cremore Rd. 11	J 4 23
Cremorne 14	F16 53
Crescent Gdns. 7	M 7 36
Crescent Pl. 3	N 6 37
Crescent Vill. 9	K 6 35
Crescent, The 9	M 4 24
Crescent, The, Donnybrook 4	M12 50
Crestfield Av. 9	L 3 24
Crestfield Clo. 9	L 3 24
Crestfield Dr. 9	L 3 24
Crestfield Pk. 9	L 3 24
Crestfield Clo.	
Croaghpatrick Rd. 7	F 6 33
Crofton Av., D.L.	U16 60
Crofton Rd., D.L.	U15 60
Crofton Ter., D.L.	U15 60
Croker La. 8	H 9 42
Cromcastle Av. 5	O 2 25
Cromcastle Dr. 5	O 2 25
Cromcastle Grn. 5	O 2 25
Cromcastle Pk. 5	O 2 25
Cromcastle Rd. 5	O 2 25
Cromwells Fort Rd. 12	D12 46
Cromwells Quarters 8	G 9 42
Cross & Passion College 9	M14 56
Cross Av., Blackrock	P14 58
Cross Av., D.L.	U16 60
Cross Guns Bridge	J 6 35
Cross Kevin St. 8	K10 43
Crosthwaite Pk. E., D.L.	V17 61
Crosthwaite Pk. S., D.L.	V17 61
Crosthwaite Pk. W., D.L.	V17 61
Crosthwaite Ter., D.L.	V16 61
Crotty Av. 12	E12 47
Crow St. 2	K 9 43
Crown Alley 2	K 9 43
Temple Bar	
Croydon Gdns. 3	M 5 36
Croydon Grn. 3	M 6 36
Croydon Park Av. 3	M 5 36
Croydon Ter. 3	M 5 36
Crumlin Rd. 12	F11 47
Cuala Rd. 7	H 6 34
Cuckoo La. 7	J 8 43
Cuffe La. 2	K10 43
Cuffe St. 2	K10 43
Cullenswood Gdns. 6	L12 50
Cullenswood Pk. 6	L12 50
Cumberland Rd. 2	L10 44
Cumberland St. N. 1	K 7 35
Cumberland St. 1	L 9 44
Cumberland St., D.L.	U16 60
Curlew Rd. 12	E11 47
Curzon St. 8	K10 43
Custom House 1	L 8 44
Custom House Quay 1	L 8 44
Cymric Rd. 4	O 9 45
Cypress Downs 6	F15 53
Cypress Dr. 6	F16 53
Cypress Garth 6	F15 53
Cypress Gro. N. 6	F15 53
Cypress Gro. S. 6	F15 53
Cypress Grove Rd. 6	F15 53
Cypress Lawn 6	F15 53
Cypress Pk. 6	F15 53
Cypress Rd., Stillorgan	O15 57
D'Olier St. 2	K 8 43
Dale Clo., Stillorgan	O16 57
Dale Dr., Stillorgan	O16 57
Dame Ct. 2	K 9 43
Dame La. 2	K 9 43
Dame St. 2	K 9 43
Daneswell Rd. 9	K 5 35
Dangan Av. 12	F13 47
Dangan Dr. 12	F13 47
Dangan Pk. 12	F13 47
Daniel St. 8	J10 43
Danieli Dr. 5	P 4 26
Danieli Rd. 5	P 4 26
Dargle Rd. 9	K 6 35
Darley St. 6	J11 49
Darleys Ter. 8	H10 43
Darling Estate 7	E 5 33
Dartmouth La. 6	L11 50
Dartmouth Pl. 6	K11 49
Dartmouth Rd. 6	K11 49
Dartmouth Sq. 6	L11 50
Dartmouth Ter. 6	K11 49
Dartry Cotts. 6	K14 55
Dartry Pk. 6	K13 49
Dartry Rd. 6	K13 49
David Pk. 9	K 6 35
David Rd. 9	K 6 35
Davis Pl. 8	J 9 43
Thomas Davis St. S.	
Davitt Rd. 12	F10 41
Dawson Ct. 2	K 9 43
Stephen St.	
Dawson La. 2	L 9 44
Dawson St. 2	K 9 43
De Courcy Sq. 9	J 5 35
De Val Av., Kilbarrack	U 3 28
De Vesci Ter., D.L.	U16 60
Deaf & Dumb Institution 7	G 6 34
Dean St. 8	J 9 43
Dean Swift Grn. 11	K 3 23
Dean Swift Rd. 11	J 3 23
Dean Swift Sq. 8	J 9 43
Swifts Alley	
Deans Grange Rd., Stillorgan	S16 59
Deanstown Av. 11	F 3 21
Deanstown Grn. 11	F 3 21
Deanstown Pk. 11	F 3 21
Deanstown Rd. 11	F 3 21
Decies Rd. 10	C 9 40
Deerpark Av., Castleknock	C 5 32
Deerpark Clo., Castleknock	C 5 32
Deerpark Dr., Castleknock	C 5 32
Deerpark Lawn, Castleknock	C 5 32
Deerpark Rd., Castleknock	C 5 32
Deerpark Rd., Stillorgan	O15 57
Delville Rd. 11	J 3 23
Delvin Rd. 7	H 6 34
Demesne 5	P 5 38
Denmark St. Gt. 1	K 7 35
Denzille La. 2	L 9 44
Denzille Pl. 2	L 9 44
Denzille La.	
Department of Defence 7	G 8 42
Infirmary Rd.	
Department of Defence 9	K 5 35
St. Mobhi Rd.	
Dermot O'Hurley Av. 4	N 9 45
Derravaragh Rd. 6	G13 48
Derry Dr. 12	F12 47
Derry Pk. 12	F12 47
Derry Rd. 12	F12 47
Derrynane Gdns. 4	N10 45
Derrynane Par. 7	K 7 35
Desmond Av., D.L.	U16 60
Desmond St. 8	J10 43
Devenish Rd. 12	G12 48
Deverell Pl. 1	L 8 44
Devoy Rd. 8	F10 41
Digges La. 2	K 9 43
Stephen St.	
Digges St. 2	K10 43
Digges St. Lwr. 2	K10 43
Cuffe La.	
Dingle Rd. 7	G 6 34
Dispensary La. 14	J16 55
Distillery Rd. 3	L 6 36
Dock Pl. S. 4	M 9 44
Dock St. S.	
Dock St. S. 4	M 9 44
Dodder Dale 14	H15 54
Dodder Park Dr. 14	H14 54
Lower Dodder Rd.	
Dodder Park Gro. 14	J14 55
Dodder Park Rd. 14	J14 55
Dodder Ter. 4	N 9 45
Doddervale 6	K14 55
Dollymount Av. 3	R 6 39
Dollymount Gro. 3	R 6 39
Dollymount Pk. 3	R 6 39
Dollymount Ri. 3	R 6 39
Dolphin Av. 8	H10 42
Dolphin Market 8	H10 42
Dolphins Barn St.	
Dolphin Rd. 12	G10 42
Dolphins Barn 8	H10 42
Dolphins Barn St. 8	H10 42
Dominican Convent 7	F 5 33
Dominick La. 1	K 8 43
Dominick Pl. 1	K 8 43
Dominick St. Lwr.	L 8 44
Dominick St. Upr. 7	J 7 35
Dominick St., D.L.	U16 60
Domville Dr. 12	F15 53
Domville Rd. 12	F15 53
Donaghmede Av. 5	T 2 28
Donaghmede Dr. 5	T 2 28
Donaghmede Pk. 5	T 2 28
Donaghmede Rd. 5	S 2 27
Donard Rd. 12	E11 47
Donelan Av. 8	G 9 42
Donnybrook Rd. 4	M12 50
Donnycarney Rd. 9	N 5 37
Donore Av. 8	H10 42
Donore Rd. 8	H10 42
Donore Ter. 8	J10 43
South Circular Rd.	
Donovans La. 8	J10 43
Clanbrassil St. Lwr.	
Doon Av. 7	H 7 34
Doris St. 4	N 9 45
Dornden Pk., Booterstown	P13 63
Dorset La. 1	K 7 35
Dorset Pl. 1	K 7 35
Dorset St. Lwr.	
Dorset St. Lwr. 1	K 7 35
Dorset St. Upr. 1	K 7 35
Dowkers La. 8	J10 43
Dowland Rd. 12	E12 47
Dowlings Ct. 2	L 9 44
Lombard St. E.	
Dowlings Ct. S. 2	L 9 44
Lombard St. E.	
Downpatrick Rd. 12	G11 48
Dowth Av. 7	H 6 34
Drapier Grn. 11	J 3 23
Drapier Rd. 11	J 3 23
Drimnagh Castle 12	D11 46
Drimnagh Rd. 12	E11 47
Dromard Rd. 12	E11 47
Dromawling Rd. 9	N 3 25
Drombawn Av. 9	N 3 25
Dromeen Av. 9	N 3 25
Dromlee Cres. 9	N 3 25
Drommartin Castle 14	M16 56
Dromnanane Pk. 9	N 3 25
Dromnanane Rd. 9	N 3 25
Dromore Rd. 12	F11 47
Drumalee Av. 7	H 7 34
Drumalee Rd.	
Drumalee Ct. 7	H 7 34
Drumalee Rd.	
Drumalee Dr. 7	H 7 34
Drumalee Rd.	
Drumalee Gro. 7	H 7 34
Drumalee Rd.	
Drumalee Pk. 7	H 7 34
Drumalee Rd. 7	H 7 34
Drumcliffe Dr. 7	G 6 34
Drumcliffe Rd. 7	G 6 34
Drumcondra Hospital 3	K 6 35
Drumcondra Rd.	L 6 36
Drumcondra Rd. Lwr. 9	K 6 35
Drumcondra Rd. Upr. 9	L 5 36
Drummartin Clo. 14	N16 57
Drummartin Cres. 14	N16 57
Drummartin Rd. 14	N16 57
Drummartin Ter. 14	N16 57
Drummond Pl. 6	J11 49
Mount Drummond Av.	
Drury St. 2	K 9 43
Dublin Corporation Food Market 7	J 8 43
St. Michans St.	
Dublin Health Authority 8	H 9 42
Dublin Rd., Kilbarrack	V 3 29
Dublin St., Baldoyle	V 2 29
Dufferin Av. 8	J10 43
Duggan Pl. 6	K12 49
Rathmines Rd.	
Duke La. Lwr. 2	K 9 43
Duke St.	
Duke La. 2	K 9 43
Duke Row 1	L 7 36
North Circular Rd.	
Duke St. 2	K 9 43
Dunard Av. 7	G 6 34
Dunard Ct. 7	G 7 34
Dunard Dr. 7	G 7 34
Dunard Pk. 7	G 7 34
Dunard Rd. 7	G 7 34
Dunard Wk. 7	G 7 34
Dundaniel Rd. 5	N 2 25
Dundela Av., D.L.	W17 61
Dundela Cres., D.L.	W17 61
Dundela Pk., D.L.	W17 61
Dundrum Rd. 14	L16 56
Dunedin Ter., D.L.	T17 60
Dungar Ter., D.L.	V16 61
Northumberland Av.	
Dungriffan Rd., Howth	BB3 31
Dunleary Hill, D.L.	U16 60
Dunleary Rd., D.L.	U15 60
Dunluce Rd. 3	P 5 38
Dunmanus Rd. 7	G 6 34
Dunne St. 1	L 7 36
Dunree Pk. 5	Q 2 26
Dunseverick Rd. 3	P 5 38
Dunsink Av. 11	F 3 21
Dunsink Dr. 11	F 3 21
Dunsink Gdns. 11	G 3 22
Dunsink Grn. 11	G 3 22
Dunsink La., Castleknock	Y 4 30

Street	Grid	Page
Dunsink Observatory	AA3	31
Dunsink Pk. 11	F 3	21
Dunsink Rd. 11	G 3	22
Dunville Av. 6	L12	50
Dunville Ter. 6	K11	49
Mountpleasant Av. Upr.		
Durham Rd. 4	O11	51
Durrow Rd. 12	G12	48
Eagle Hill Av. 6	H13	48
Earl Pl. 1	K 8	43
Earl St. N. 1	K 8	43
Earl St. S. 8	J 9	43
Earlsfort Mans. 2	K10	43
Adelaide Rd.		
Earlsfort Ter. 2	K10	43
East Oil Jetty	P 9	62
East Rd. 3	M 8	44
East Wall Rd. 3	M 7	36
Eastern Breakwater 1	P 9	62
Eastmoreland La. 4	M10	44
Eastmoreland Pl. 4	M10	44
Eaton Brae 14	K14	55
Eaton Pl., D.L.	S15	59
Eaton Rd. 6	H13	48
Eaton Sq. 6	H13	48
Eaton Sq., D.L.	S15	59
Ebenezer Ter. 8	H10	42
Eblana Av., D.L.	V16	61
Eblana Vill. 2	M 9	44
Eccles Pl. 1	K 7	35
Eccles St. 7	K 7	35
Echlin St. 8	H 9	42
Eden Park Dr. 14	N16	57
Eden Park Rd. 14	N16	57
Eden Pk., D.L.	V17	61
Eden Quay 1	K 8	43
Eden Rd. Lwr., D.L.	V17	61
Eden Rd. Upr., D.L.	V17	61
Eden Ter., D.L.	V17	61
Eden Vill., D.L.	V17	61
Edenbrook Dr. 14	G16	54
Edenbrook Pk. 14	G16	54
Edenmore Av. 5	Q 3	26
Edenmore Cres. 5	R 3	27
Edenmore Cres. 5	R 3	27
Edenmore Dr. 5	R 3	27
Edenmore Gdns. 5	R 3	27
Edenmore Grn. 5	R 3	27
Edenmore Grn. 5	R 3	27
Edenmore Gro. 5	R 3	27
Edenmore Pk. 5	Q 3	26
Edenvale Rd. 6	L12	50
Effra Rd. 6	J12	49
Eglinton Ct. 4	M12	50
Eglinton Pk. 4	M12	50
Eglinton Pk., D.L.	V16	61
Eglinton Rd. 4	M12	50
Eglinton Ter. 14	M16	56
Eglinton Ter. 4	M12	50
Eldon Ter. 8	J10	43
South Circular Rd.		
Elgin Rd. 4	M11	50
Elizabeth St. 3	L 6	36
Ellenfield Rd. 9	M 3	24
Ellesmere Av. 7	H 7	34
Ellis Quay 7	H 8	42
Elliss St. 7	H 8	42
Benburb St.		
Elm Gro., D.L.	R16	59
Elm Grove Cotts. 7	E 6	33
Blackhorse Av.		
Elm Mount Av. 9	N 4	25
Elm Mount Clo. 9	N 4	25
Elm Mount Cres. 5	N 3	25
Elm Mount Ct. 9	O 4	25
Elm Mount Dr. 9	N 4	25
Elm Mount Gro. 9	N 3	25
Elm Mount Heights 9	N 3	25
Elm Mount Lawn 9	N 3	25
Elm Mount Pk. 9	N 4	25
Elm Mount Ri. 9	N 4	25
Elm Mount Vw. 9	N 4	25
Elm Rd. 9	N 4	25
Elmpark Av. 6	L11	50
Elmpark Ter. 6	H13	48
Elmpark Ter., Ranelagh 6	L11	50
Elms, The 4	O13	51
Elms, The, D.L.	Q15	58
Elmwood Av. 6	L11	50
Elmwood Av. Upr. 6	L11	50
Elton Ct. 5	R 2	27
Elton Dr.		
Elton Pk. 5	R 2	27
Elton Pk., D.L.	W17	61
Elton Wk. 5	R 2	27
Elton Dr.		
Ely Pl. 2	L10	44
Ely Pl. Upr. 2	L10	44
Embassy Lawn 14	M14	56
Emerald Cotts. 4	M10	44
Grand Canal St. Upr.		
Emerald Pl. 1	M 8	44
Sheriff St. Lwr.		
Emerald Sq. 8	H10	42
Emerald St. 1	M 8	44
Emily Pl. 1	L 8	44
Sheriff St. Lwr.		
Emmet Rd. 8	F 9	41
Emmet Sq., D.L.	Q14	58
Emmet St. 1	L 7	36
Emmet St., Haroldscross 6	J11	49
Emor St. 8	J10	43
Emorville Av. 8	J10	43
Emorville Sq. 8	J10	43
South Circular Rd.		
Empress Pl. 1	L 7	36
Enaville Rd. 3	M 7	36
Engine Alley 8	J 9	43
Ennafort Av. 5	Q 4	26
(Ascal Dun Eanna)		
Ennafort Dr. 5	Q 4	26
(Ceide Dun Eanna)		
Ennafort Gro. 5	Q 4	26
Ennafort Pk. 5	Q 4	26
Ennafort Rd. 5	Q 4	26
Ennel Rd. 5	Q 3	26
Enniskerry Rd. 7	J 6	35
Erne Pl. 2	M 9	44
Erne Pl. Lit. 2	M 9	44
Erne St. Lwr. 2	M 9	44
Erne St. Upr. 2	M 9	44
Errigal Gdns. 12	E11	47
Errigal Gdns. 12	E11	47
Errigal Rd.		
Errigal Rd. 12	E11	47
Erris Rd. 7	H 6	34
Esmond Av. 3	M 6	36
Esposito Rd. 12	E12	47
Essex Quay 8	K 9	43
Essex St. E. 2	K 9	43
Essex St. W. 8	K 9	43
Estate Av. 4	O13	51
Estate Cotts., 4	M10	44
Northumberland Rd.		
Eugene St. 8	H10	42
Eustace St. 2	K 9	43
Everton Av. 7	H 7	34
Ewington La. 8	H 9	42
Exchange Ct. 2	K 9	43
Dame St.		
Exchange St. Lwr. 8	K 9	43
Exchange St. Upr. 8	K 9	43
Cork Hill		
Exchequer St. 2	K 9	43
Fade St. 2	K 9	43
Fairbrook Lawn 14	H16	54
Fairfield Av. 3	M 7	36
Fairfield Pk. 6	J13	49
Fairfield Rd., Glasnevin 9	K 5	35
Fairlawn Pk. 11	G 4	22
Fairview 3	M 6	36
Fairview Av. Lwr. 3	M 6	36
Fairview Av. Upr. 3	M 6	36
Fairview Av., Irishtown 4	N 9	45
Fairview Grn. 3	M 6	36
Fairview Passage 3	M 6	36
Fairview Strand		
Fairview Strand 3	M 6	36
Fairview Ter. 3	M 6	36
Fairways, 11	M 7	36
Faith Av. 3	M 7	36
Falcarragh Rd. 9	L 3	24
Farmhill Dr. 14	M15	56
Farmhill Pk. 14	M16	56
Farmhill Rd. 14	M15	56
Farney Pk. 4	O10	45
Farnham Cres. 11	G 3	22
Farnham Pk. 11	G 3	22
Farrenboley Cotts. 14	L14	56
Farrenboley Pk. 14	L14	56
Father Matthew Bridge	J 9	43
Fatima Mans. 8	G10	42
Faughart Rd. 12	G12	48
Faussagh Av. 7	G 6	34
Faussagh Rd. 7	H 6	34
Fenian St. 2	L 9	44
Fergus Rd. 6	H14	54
Ferguson Rd. 9	K 5	35
Ferndale Av. 11	H 3	22
Ferndale Rd. 11	H 3	22
Fernhill Av. 12	E14	53
Fernhill Pk. 12	E14	53
Fernhill Rd. 12	E14	53
Ferns Rd. 12	G12	48
Fernvale Dr. 12	F11	47
Ferrard Rd. 6	J13	49
Fertullagh Rd. 7	H 6	34
Field Av. 12	E12	47
Fields Ter. 6	L11	50
Ranelagh		
Fifth Av. 8	G10	42
Findlater Pl. 1	K 8	43
Findlater St., D.L.	V17	61
Findlaters St. 7	G 8	42
Fingal Av. 3	Q 6	38
Clontarf		
Fingal Pl. 7	H 7	34
Fingal St. 8	H10	42
Finglas Bridge	H 4	22
Finglas Pk. 11	H 2	22
Finglas Pl. 11	G 3	22
Finglas Rd. 11	G 3	22
Finglas Rd. Old 11	J 4	23
Finsbury Pk. 14	L16	56
First Av. 1	M 8	44
First Av., Inchicore 10	D 9	40
Fishamble St. 8	J 9	43
Fitzgerald Pk., D.L.	U17	60
Fitzgerald St. 6	J11	49
Fitzgibbon La. 1	L 7	36
Fitzgibbon St. 1	L 7	36
Fitzmaurice Rd. 11	J 3	23
Fitzroy Av. 3	L 6	36
Fitzwilliam La. 2	L10	44
Fitzwilliam Pl. 2	L10	44
Fitzwilliam Quay 4	N 9	45
Fitzwilliam Sq. E. 2	L10	44
Fitzwilliam Sq. N. 2	L10	44
Fitzwilliam Sq. S. 2	L10	44
Fitzwilliam Sq. W. 2	L10	44
Fitzwilliam St. Lwr. 2	L10	44
Fitzwilliam St. Upr. 2	L10	44
Fitzwilliam St., Ringsend 4	N 9	45
Fleet St. 2	K 9	43
Fleming Rd. 9	K 5	35
Flemings La. 4	M10	44
Haddington Rd.		
Flemings Pl. 4	L10	44
Floraville Rd., Donnybrook 4	M12	50
Florence St. 8	K11	49
Lennox St.		
Foley St. 1	L 8	44
Fontenoy St. 7	J 7	35
Fonthill Pk. 14	H16	54
Fonthill Rd. 14	H16	54
Forbes La. 8	H 9	42
Forbes St. 2	M 9	44
Fortfield Dr. 6	G14	54
Fortfield Dr. 6	G15	54
Fortfield Gdns. 6	K13	49
Fortfield Gro. 6	G14	54
Fortfield Pk. 6	G15	54
Fortfield Ter. 6	K13	49
Forth Rd. 3	N 7	37
Fortview Av. 3	Q 7	38
Foster Cotts. 7	J 7	35
Phibsborough Rd.		
Foster Pl. S. 2	K 9	43
Foster Ter. 3	L 7	36
Fosters Av., Stillorgan	O15	57
Fosters, The, Stillorgan	O15	57
Fountain Pl. 7	J 8	43
Fourth Av. 1	M 8	44
Fourth Av. 8	G10	42
Fownes St. 2	K 9	43
Foxfield Av. 5	S 3	27
Foxfield Cres. 5	T 3	28
Foxfield Dr. 5	T 3	28
Foxfield Grn. 5	T 3	28
Foxfield Gro. 5	Q 3	27
Foxfield Heights 5	S 3	27
Foxfield Lawn 5	T 3	28
Foxfield Rd. 5	T 4	28
Foxfield Rd. 5	S 3	27
Foxfield St. John 5	T 3	28
Foxhill Av. 5	R 2	27
Foxhill Clo. 5	R 2	27
Foxhill Cres. 5	R 2	27
Foxhill Ct. 5	R 2	27
Foxhill Dr. 5	R 2	27
Foxhill Grn. 5	R 2	27
Foxhill Gro. 5	R 2	27
Foxhill Lawn 5	R 2	27
Foxhill Pk. 5	R 2	27
Foxhill Way 5	R 2	27
Foxs La. 5	T 4	28
Foyle Rd. 3	M 6	36
Francis St. 8	J 9	43
Frankfort Av. 6	K13	49
Frankfort Castle 14	L15	56
Frankfort Pk. 14	L15	56
Frascati Pk., D.L.	R15	59
Frascati Rd., D.L.	R15	59
Frederick Ct. N. 1	K 7	35
Frederick La. N. 1	K 7	35
Frederick La. 2	L 9	44
Frederick St. N. 1	K 7	35
Frederick St. S. 2	L 9	44
Frenchmans La. 1	L 8	44
Gardiner St. Lwr.		
Friarsland Av. 14	M15	56
Friarsland Rd. 14	M15	56
Friary Av. 7	J 8	43

Name	Grid
Fumballys La. 8	J10 43
Furry Park Rd. 5	Q5 38
Furry Pk. 5	P5 38
Gaelic St. 3	M7 36
Gairdini Sheinleasa 9	K2 23
Galmoy Rd. 11	H6 34
Galtymore Clo. 12	E10 41
Galtymore Dr. 12	F10 41
Galtymore Pk. 12	E11 47
Galtymore Rd. 12	E11 47
Garden La. 8	J9 43
Gardiner Pl. 1	K7 35
Gardiner Row 1	K7 35
Gardiner St. Lwr. 1	L7 36
Gardiner St. Mid. 1	L7 36
Gardiner St. Upr. 1	K7 35
Gardiners La. 1	L7 36
Gardiners Row, D.L.	P14 58
Gardini Lein 5	Q4 26
(Lein Gdns.)	
Gardini Phairc An Bhailtini 7	F6 33
(Villa Park Gdns.)	
Garriglea Gdns., D.L.	U17 60
Garryowen Rd. 10	C9 40
Gartan Av. 9	K6 35
Garville Av. 6	J13 49
Garville Av. Upr. 6	J13 49
Garville Rd. 6	J13 49
Geoffrey Keating Rd. 8	J10 43
O'Curry Rd.	
Georges Av., D.L.	R15 59
Georges Hill 7	J8 43
Georges La. 7	J8 43
Georges Pl. 1	K7 35
Georges Pl., D.L.	R15 59
Georges Pl., D.L.	U16 60
Georges Quay 2	L8 44
Georges St. Lwr., D.L.	U16 60
Georges St. Upr., D.L.	V16 61
Gerald St. 4	M9 44
Geraldine St. 7	J7 35
Geraldine Ter. 6	L13 50
Gilbert Rd. 8	J10 43
Gilford Av. 4	O11 51
Gilford Dr. 4	O11 51
Gilford Pk. 4	O11 51
Gilford Rd. 4	O11 51
Glanarriff Rd., Ashtown	E5 33
Glandore Pk., D.L.	U17 60
Glandore Rd. 9	M5 36
Glansanaon Rd. 11	H3 22
Glasaree Rd. 11	H3 22
Glasgow Ct. 14	L14 56
Glasilawn Av. 11	J4 23
Glasilawn Rd. 11	H4 22
Glasmeen Rd. 11	H4 22
Glasnamana Pl. 11	J4 23
Glasnamana Rd. 11	H4 22
Glasnevin Av. 11	H2 22
Glasnevin Bridge	K5 35
Glasnevin Ct. 11	H4 22
Glasnevin Dr. 11	J3 23
Glasnevin Hill 9	K5 35
Glasnevin Pk. 11	J2 23
Glasthule Rd., D.L.	W17 61
Gledswood Av. 14	M14 56
Gledswood Clo. 14	M14 56
Gledswood Pk. 14	M14 56
Glenaan Rd. 9	L3 24
Glenabbey Rd., Stillorgan	O16 57
Glenageary Rd. Lwr., D.L.	V17 61
Glenageary Rd. Upr., D.L.	U17 60
Glenageary Station, D.L.	W17 61
Glenageary Woods, D.L.	U17 60
Glenanne 12	G13 48
Glenard Av. 7	H7 34
Glenarm Av. 9	L6 36
Glenart Av., D.L.	Q16 58
Glenaulin Dr., Chapelizod	C8 40
(Ceide Gleannaluinn)	
Glenavy Pk. 6	G13 48
Glenayle Rd. 5	R2 27
Glenayr Rd. 6	J14 55
Glenbeigh Pk. 7	G7 34
Glenbeigh Rd. 7	G7 34
Glenbower Pk. 14	L16 56
Glenbrook Pk. 14	H16 54
Glenbrook Rd. 7	E6 33
Glencar Rd. 7	G7 34
Glenciloy Rd. 9	L3 24
Glencorp Rd. 9	M3 24
Glendale Pk. 12	F14 53
Glendalough Rd. 9	K6 35
Glendhu Pk., Ashtown	E5 33
Glendhu Rd., Ashtown	E5 33
Glendoo Clo. 12	C14 52
Lugnaquilla Av.	
Glendown Av. 12	E14 53
Glendown Clo. 12	E14 53
Glendown Gro.	
Glendown Cres. 12	E14 53
Glendown Ct. 12	E14 53
Glendown Grn. 12	E14 53
Glendown Gro.	
Glendown Gro. 12	E14 53
Glendown Lawn 12	F14 53
Glendown Pk. 12	E14 53
Glendown Rd. 12	F14 53
Glendun Rd. 9	H11 48
Glenealy Rd. 12	H11 48
Glenfarne Rd. 5	Q2 26
Glengara Pk., D.L.	V17 61
Glengariff Pk. 7	K6 35
Glenhill Av. 11	H3 22
Glenhill Ct. 11	H3 22
Glenhill Dr. 11	H3 22
Glenhill Gro. 11	H3 22
Glenhill Pk. 11	H3 22
Glenhill Vill. 11	H3 22
Glenmalure Pk. 8	G10 42
Glenmore Rd. 7	G7 34
Glenomena Gro., Booterstown	O14 57
Glenomena Pk., Booterstown	O13 51
Glenties Dr. 11	F4 21
Glenties Pk. 11	F4 21
Glentow Rd. 9	L3 24
Glentworth Pk. 5	R2 27
Slademore Av.	
Glenview Lawns, Tallaght	D16 52
Glenview Pk., Tallaght	C16 52
Glenwood Rd. 5	Q3 26
Gloucester La. 1	K8 43
Sean McDermott St.	
Gloucester Pl. 1	L7 36
Gloucester Pl. Lwr.	L8 44
Railway Pl.	
Gloucester Pl. Lwr. 1	L8 44
Gloucester Pl. Upr. 1	L7 36
Gloucester St. S. 2	L8 44
Gloucester Ter. 1	L7 36
Glovers Alley 2	K9 43
Goatstown Av. 14	M15 56
Goatstown Rd. 14	N15 57
Golden Bridge 8	E9 41
Golden La. 8	K9 43
Goldenbridge Av. 8	F10 41
Goldenbridge Gdns. 8	F10 41
Goldenbridge Ter. 8	E9 41
Connolly Av.	
Goldsmith St. 7	J7 35
Gordon St. 4	M9 44
Gorsefield Ct. 5	Q3 26
Gortbeg Av. 11	G4 22
Gortbeg Rd.	
Gortbeg Dr. 11	G4 22
Gortbeg Rd.	
Gortbeg Pk. 11	G4 22
Gortbeg Rd.	
Gortbeg Rd. 11	G4 22
Gortmore Av. 11	G4 22
Gortmore Dr. 11	G4 22
Gortmore Pk. 11	G4 22
Gortmore Rd.	
Gortmore Rd. 11	G4 22
Government Building 2	L9 44
Gowrie Pk., D.L.	U17 60
Grace O'Malley Dr.	AA3 31
Grace O'Malley Rd., Howth	AA3 31
Grace Park Av. 3	L6 36
Grace Park Gdns. 9	L5 36
Grace Park Heights 9	M4 24
Grace Park Rd. 9	L5 36
Grace Park Ter. 9	M5 36
Gracefield Av. 5	Q4 26
Gracefield Rd. 5	P4 26
Gracefield, D.L.	Q15 58
Grafton St. 2	K9 43
Graham St. 1	K7 35
Granby La. 1	K7 35
Granby Pl. 1	K8 43
Granby Row 1	K7 35
Grand Canal Bank 8	G10 42
Grand Canal Bank, Ranelagh 6	K11 49
Grand Canal Harbour 8	H9 42
Jamess St	
Grand Canal Pl. N. 8	H9 42
Grand Canal Quay 2	M9 44
Grand Canal St. Lwr. 2	M9 44
Grand Canal St. Upr. 4	M10 44
Grand Par. 6	K11 49
Grange Park Av. 5	S3 27
Grange Park Clo. 5	S3 27
Grange Park Cres. 5	S3 27
Grange Park Dr. 5	S3 27
Grange Park Grn. 5	S3 27
Grange Park Gro. 5	S3 27
Grange Park Par. 5	S3 27
Grange Park Rd. 5	S3 27
Grange Park Ri. 5	S3 27
Grange Park Wk. 5	S3 27
Grange Pk. 14	H16 54
Grange Rd. 14	H16 54
Grange Rd. 5	S3 27
Grange Rd., Raheny 5	R4 27
Grangegorman Lwr. 7	J8 43
Grangegorman Upr. 7	J7 35
Grangemore Av. 5	S2 27
Grangemore Ct. 5	S2 27
Rosapenna Dr.	
Grangemore Gro. 5	S2 27
Grangemore Pk. 5	S2 27
Rosapenna Dr.	
Grangemore Ri. 5	S2 27
Rosapenna Dr.	
Granite Ter. 8	E9 41
Inchicore Ter. S.	
Grantham Pl. 8	K10 43
Grantham St. 8	K10 43
Grants Row 2	M9 44
Grattan Cres. 8	E9 41
Grattan Par. 9	K6 35
Grattan St. 2	M9 44
Gray Sq. 8	J9 43
Pimlico	
Gray St. 8	J9 43
Great Clarence Pl. 2	M9 44
Great Western Av. 7	J7 35
North Circular Rd.	
Great Western Sq. 7	J7 35
Great Western Vill. 7	J7 35
Greek St. 7	J8 43
Green Pk. 14	K14 55
Green Rd., D.L.	Q15 58
Green St. 7	J8 43
Green St. E. 2	N9 45
Green St. Lit. 7	J8 43
Greenacre Ct. 14	E16 53
Greencastle Av. 5	P2 26
Greencastle Cres. 5	P2 26
Greencastle Dr. 5	P2 26
Greencastle Par. 5	Q2 26
Greendale Av. 5	T3 28
Greendale Rd. 5	T3 28
Greenfield Cres. 4	N13 51
Greenfield Pk. 4	N13 51
Greenfield Rd., Stillorgan	P15 58
Greenhills Rd., Tallaght	C15 52
Greenlea Av. 6	G14 54
Greenlea Dr. 6	G14 54
Greenlea Gro. 6	G14 54
Greenlea Pk. 6	G14 54
Greenlea Rd. 6	G14 54
Greenmount Av. 12	J11 49
Greenmount Ct. 12	J11 49
Greenmount Av.	
Greenmount La. 12	J11 49
Greenmount Lawns 6	H14 54
Greenmount Rd. 6	J13 49
Greenmount Sq. 12	J11 49
Greenmount La.	
Greenore Ter. 2	M9 44
Greentrees Dr. 12	E14 53
Greentrees Pk. 12	E13 47
Greentrees Rd. 12	E14 53
Grenville Av. 8	J10 43
Grenville Rd., D.L.	S16 59
Grenville Ter. 8	J10 43
Grenville La. 1	K7 35
Grenville St. 1	K7 35
Gresham Ter., D.L.	V16 61
Greygates, D.L.	P15 58
Greyhound Race Track 6	J12 49
Greys La., Howth	BB4 31
Greythorn Pk., D.L.	V17 61
Griffith Av. 9	K6 23
Griffith Av. Ext. 11	J4 23
Griffith Ct. 9	M5 36
Griffith Downs 9	L4 24
Griffith Dr. 11	H3 22
Griffith Lawns 9	K4 23
Griffith Par. 11	H4 22
Griffith Sq. S. 8	J10 43
South Circular Rd.	
Grosvenor Ct. 12	F14 53
Grosvenor Pl. 6	J12 49
Grosvenor Rd. 6	J12 49
Grosvenor Sq. 6	J12 49
Grosvenor Ter., D.L.	U16 60
Grosvenor Vill. 6	J12 49
Grotto Av., Booterstown	P14 58
Grotto Pl., Booterstown	P14 58
Grove Av. 6	J11 49
Grove Rd.	
Grove Av., Blackrock	Q15 58
Grove Av., Finglas 11	H2 22
Grove Lawn, Stillorgan	Q15 58
Grove Park Av. 11	H2 22
Grove Park Cres. 11	J2 23
Grove Park Pk. 11	H2 22
Grove Park Rd. 11	H2 22
Grove Pk. 6	K11 49
Grove Rd., Finglas 11	H2 22
Grove Rd., Rathmines 6	J11 49
Grove, The 9	M4 24
Grovewood 11	H2 22

Name	Ref
Guild St. 1	M 8 44
Guinness Brewery 8	H 9 42
Gulistan Cotts. 6	K11 49
Gulistan Pl. 6	K12 49
Gulistan Ter. 6	K11 49
H.S. Reilly Bridge	F 5 33
Haddington Pl. 4	M10 44
Haddington Rd. 4	M10 44
Haddington Ter., D.L.	V16 61
Haddon Pk. 3	O 6 37
Seaview Av. N.	
Haddon Rd. 3	O 6 37
Haigh Ter., D.L.	V16 61
Halliday Rd. 7	H 8 42
Halliday Sq. 7	H 8 42
Halston St. 7	J 8 43
Hamilton St. 8	H10 42
Hammond La. 7	J 8 43
Hammond St. 8	J10 43
Hampstead Av. 9	K 4 23
Hampstead Ct. 9	K 3 23
Hampstead Pk. 9	K 4 23
Hampton Convent 9	M 5 36
Hampton Estate 3	Q 5 38
Hanbury La. 8	J 9 43
Hannaville Pk. 6	H13 48
Hanover La. 8	J 9 43
Hanover Quay 2	M 9 44
Hanover Sq. W. 8	J 9 43
Hanover La.	
Hanover St. E. 2	L 9 44
Hanover St. W. 8	J 9 43
Park St. W.	
Harbour Ct. 1	K 8 43
Marlborough St.	
Harbour Ter., D.L.	U15 60
Harcourt La. 2	K10 43
Harcourt Rd.	
Harcourt Rd. 2	K10 43
Harcourt St. 2	K10 43
Harcourt Ter. 2	L10 44
Hardbeck Av. 12	D12 46
Hardiman Rd. 9	K 5 35
Hardwicke Pl. 1	K 7 35
Hardwicke St. 1	K 7 35
Harlech Cres. 14	N15 57
Harlech Gro. 14	N15 57
Harlech Vill. 14	N15 57
Harman St. 8	H10 42
Harmonstown Gro. 5	Q 4 26
Harmonstown Rd. 5	Q 4 26
Harmony Av. 4	M12 50
Harmony Row 2	M 9 44
Harold Rd. 7	H 8 42
Harolds Cross 6	J11 49
Harolds Cross Rd. 6	H13 48
Haroldville Av. 8	H10 42
Harrington St. 8	K10 43
Harrison Row 4	J13 49
Harry Av. 12	E12 47
Harty Pl. 8	J10 43
Harvard 14	N15 57
Hastings St. 4	N 9 45
Hatch La. 2	L10 44
Hatch St. Lwr. 2	L10 44
Hatch St. Upr. 2	K10 43
Havelock Sq. E. 4	N10 45
Havelock Sq. N. 4	N10 45
Havelock Sq. S. 4	N10 45
Havelock Sq. W. 4	N10 45
Havelock Ter. 4	N10 45
Bath Av.	
Haverty Rd. 3	N 6 37
Hawkins St. 2	L 8 44
Hawthorn Av. 3	M 8 44
Church Rd.	
Hawthorn Ter. 3	M 7 36
Haymarket 7	J 8 43
Hazel Rd. 9	N 5 37
Hazelbrook Dr. 6	G13 48
Hazelbrook Rd. 6	G13 48
Hazelcroft Gdns. 11	G 4 22
Hazelcroft Rd.	
Hazelcroft Pk. 12	G 4 22
Hazelcroft Rd.	
Hazelcroft Rd. 11	G 4 22
Hazelwood Dr. 5	O 3 25
Hazelwood Gro. 5	O 3 25
Hazelwood Pk. 5	O 3 25
Headford Gro. 14	K16 55
Healthfield Rd. 6	J13 49
Healy St. 1	K 7 35
Mountjoy Sq.	
Heath Cres. 7	E 5 33
Heath Gro. 7	F 5 33
Heidelberg 14	N15 57
Hendrick La. 7	H 8 42
Benburb St.	
Hendrick Pl. 8	H 8 42
Hendrick St. 7	J 8 43
Henley Pk. 14	L15 56
Henley Vill. 14	L15 56
Henrietta La. 1	K 8 43
Henrietta Pl. 1	J 8 43
Henrietta St. 1	J 8 43
Henry Pl. 1	K 8 43
Henry St. 1	K 8 43
Herbert Av. 4	P13 63
Herbert Cotts. 4	N11 51
Herbert Pk. 4	M11 50
Herbert Pl. 2	M10 44
Herbert Rd. 4	N10 45
Herbert St. 2	L10 44
Herberton Dr. 12	G10 42
Herberton Pk. 8	G10 42
Heuston Station 8	G 8 42
Hewardine Ter. 1	L 7 36
Killarney St.	
Heytesbury La. 4	M11 50
Heytesbury Pl. 8	J10 43
Long La.	
Heytesbury St. 8	K10 43
Hibernian Av. 3	M 7 36
Hibernian Marino School 3	R 6 39
High School of Domestic Economy, D.L.	Q14 58
High St. 8	J 9 43
Highfield Gro. 6	K13 49
Highfield Pk. 14	L15 56
Highfield Rd. 6	J13 49
Highthorn Pk., D.L.	U17 60
Hill St. 1	K 7 35
Hill, The, D.L.	U16 60
Hillcrest Pk. 11	J 3 23
Hillsbrook Av. 12	E13 47
Hillsbrook Cres. 12	E13 47
Hillsbrook Dr. 12	F13 47
Hillsbrook Gro. 12	E13 47
Hillside Dr. 14	J15 55
Hoeys Ct. 2	K 9 43
Castle St.	
Hogan Av. 2	M 9 44
Hogan Pl. 2	M 9 44
Holles Row 2	M 9 44
Holles St. 2	L 9 44
Holly Rd. 9	N 5 37
Hollybank Av. 6	L12 50
Hollybank Rd. 9	K 6 35
Hollybrook Gro. 3	N 6 37
Hollybrook Pk. 3	O 6 37
Hollybrook Rd. 3	O 6 37
Hollywood Dr. 14	N16 57
Hollywood Pk. 14	N16 57
Holmston Av., D.L.	V17 61
Holy Cross College 3	L 6 36
Holycross Av. 3	L 6 36
Holylands Dr. 14	K16 55
Holylands Rd. 14	K16 55
Holyrood Pk. 4	O11 51
Holywell Cres. 5	S 2 27
Holywell Rd. 5	S 2 27
Home Farm Pk. 9	L 5 36
Home Farm Rd. 9	K 4 23
Home Vill. 4	M11 50
Homeville 6	K12 49
Hope Av. 3	M 7 36
Hope St. 4	M 9 44
Horsemans Row 1	K 8 43
Parnell St.	
Horton Ct. 6	H14 54
Hospital for Incurables 4	L11 50
Hotel Yard 1	K 8 43
House of Retreat 8	E10 41
Howard St. 4	M 9 44
Howth Castle, Howth	AA3 31
Howth Golf Course, Howth	Z 4 30
Howth Rd. 3	N 6 37
Howth View Pk. 5	S 2 27
Howth View Pk. 5	S 2 27
Grange Rd.	
Howth Vw. 5	T 2 28
Huband Bridge	M10 44
Huband Rd. 12	D11 46
Hudson Rd., D.L.	W17 61
Hughes Rd. E. 12	E12 47
Hughes Rd. N. 12	E12 47
Hughes Rd. S. 12	E12 47
Hume St. 2	L10 44
Huttons Pl. 1	L 7 36
Huxley Cres. 8	H10 42
Hyacinth St. 3	M 7 36
Hyde Park Av., D.L.	Q15 58
Hyde Park Gdns., Blackrock	Q15 58
Hyde Pk. 6	G15 54
Idrone Ter., D.L.	R15 59
Imaal Rd. 7	H 6 34
Inchicore Rd. 8	F 9 41
Inchicore Sq. 8	F 9 41
Inchicore Ter. N. 8	E 9 41
Inchicore Ter. S. 8	E 9 41
Incorporated Dental Hospital of Ireland 2	L 9 44
Incorporated Orthopaedic Hospital of Ireland 3	P 6 38
Infirmary Rd. 7	G 8 42
Ingram Rd. 3	J10 43
Innisfallen Par. 7	K 6 35
Innishmaan Rd. 9	L 4 24
Inns Quay 8	J 9 43
Inver Rd. 7	G 6 34
Invermore Gro. 5	S 2 27
Carraroe Av.	
Inverness Rd. 3	M 6 36
Iona Cres. 9	K 6 35
Iona Dr. 9	K 6 35
Iona Pk. 9	K 6 35
Iona Rd. 9	J 6 35
Iona Vill. 9	K 6 35
Iris Gro., Stillorgan	O15 57
Irishtown Rd. 4	N 9 45
Irvine Cres. 3	M 8 44
Church Rd.	
Irvine Ter. 3	M 8 44
Irwin St. 8	G 9 42
Island St. 8	H 9 42
Island Vill. 2	M 9 44
Eblana Vill.	
Islington Av., D.L.	V16 61
Isolda Rd. 4	O 9 45
Ivar St. 7	H 8 42
Iveagh Bldgs. 8	J10 43
Iveagh Gdns. 12	F11 47
Iveleary Rd. 9	L 4 24
Iveragh Rd. 9	L 4 24
James Joyce Ct., Kilbarrack	U 3 28
James Larkin Rd. 5	S 5 39
James McCormack Gdns., Sutton	W 2 29
James Pl. E. 2	L10 44
James St. N. 3	M 7 36
Jamess Gate 8	H 9 42
Jamess St.	
Jamess St. 8	H 9 42
Jamess St. E. 2	L10 44
Jamestown Av. 8	G10 42
Jamestown Rd., Finglas 11	G 2 22
Jamestown Rd., Inchicore 8	D10 40
Jane Ville 8	J10 43
Jervis La. Lwr. 1	K 8 43
Jervis La. Upr. 1	K 8 43
Jervis St. 1	K 8 43
Jervis St. Hospital 1	K 8 43
Jetty Rd. 1	P 8 62
John Dillon St. 8	J 9 43
John F. Kennedy Dr. 12	C11 46
John McCormack Av. 12	E12 47
John St. S. 8	J 9 43
John St. W. 8	J 9 43
Johns La. W. 8	J 9 43
Johnsons Ct. 2	K 9 43
Grafton St.	
Johnsons Pl. 2	K 9 43
King St. S.	
Johnstown Pk. 11	J 3 23
Joness Rd. 3	L 7 36
Josephine Av. 7	K 7 35
Leo St.	
Joy St. 4	M 9 44
Barrow St.	
Joyce Rd. 9	K 5 35
Jumping Ground	N11 51
Kealleen Av., Tallaght	C14 52
Kearns Pl. 8	G 9 42
Keeper Rd. 12	G10 42
Kells Rd. 12	G12 48
Kellys Av., D.L.	U15 60
Kellys Row 1	K 7 35
Dorset St. Lwr.	
Kenilworth Pk. 6	H12 48
Kenilworth Rd. 6	J12 49
Kenilworth Sq. E. 6	J12 49
Kenilworth Sq. N. 6	J12 49
Kenilworth Sq. S. 6	J12 49
Kenilworth Sq. W. 6	J12 49
Kenmare Par. 1	K 7 35
Dorset St. Lwr.	
Kennedys Vill. 8	G 9 42
Kennington Clo., Tallaght	D15 52
Kennington Cres., Tallaght	D15 52
Kennington Lawn, Tallaght	E15 53
Kennington Rd., Tallaght	D15 52
Keogh Sq. 8	F 9 41
Kerlogue Rd. 4	O10 45
Kevin St. Lwr. 8	K10 43
Kevin St. Upr. 8	J10 43
Kickam Rd. 8	F 9 41
Kilakea Clo. 12	C14 52
Tibradden Dr.	
Kilakea Dr. 12	C14 52
Tibradden Dr.	
Kilbarrack Av. 5	U 3 28
Kilbarrack Gdns. 5	U 3 28
Kilbarrack Gro. 5	T 3 28
Kilbarrack Rd. 5	S 2 27

Name	Grid	Page
Kilbarron Av. 5	N 2	25
Kilbarron Dr. 5	N 2	25
Kilbarron Pk. 5	N 2	25
Kilbarron Rd. 5	N 2	25
Kilbride Rd. 5	P 5	38
Jamess St.		
Kildare Pk. 12	F11	47
Kildare Rd. 12	F11	47
Kildare St. 2	L 9	44
Kildonan Av. 11	F 2	21
Kildonan Dr. 11	F 2	21
Kildonan Rd. 11	F 2	21
Kilfenora Dr. 12	S 2	27
Kilfenora Rd. 12	G12	48
Kilkieran Rd. 7	G 5	34
Kill Av., D.L.	T17	60
Killala Rd. 7	G 5	34
Killan Rd. 3	M 8	44
Killarney Av. 1	L 7	36
Killarney Par. 7	K 6	35
Killarney St. 1	L 7	36
Killary Gro. 5	S 2	27
Ardara Av.		
Killeen Rd. 12	K12	49
Killester Abbey 5	P 4	26
Killester Av. 5	O 4	25
Killester Pk. 5	P 4	26
Killester Station 5	P 5	38
Kilmacud Pk., Stillorgan	O16	57
Kilmacud Rd. Lwr. 14	N16	57
Kilmacud Rd. Upr. 14	M16	56
Kilmainham Bridge	F 9	42
Kilmainham La. 8	F 9	41
Kilmashogue Clo. 12	D14	52
Kilmashogue Dr.		
Kilmashogue Dr. 12	D14	52
Kilmashogue Gro. 12	C14	52
Kilmore Av. 5	O 2	25
Kilmore Clo. 5	O 2	25
Kilmore Cres. 5	P 2	26
Kilmore Dr. 5	O 2	25
Kilmore Rd. 5	O 3	25
Kilmorony Clo. 5	S 2	27
Kilnamanagh Rd. 12	D12	46
Kilohan Gro. 12	D14	52
Kilshane Rd. 11	E 3	21
Kilvere 14	G15	54
Kilworth Rd. 12	E11	47
Kimmage Cross Roads	G13	48
Kimmage Rd. Lwr. 6	G13	48
Kimmage Rd. W. 12	F13	47
Kinahan St. 7	G 8	42
Kincora Av. 3	O 6	37
Kincora Ct. 3	Q 7	38
Kincora Dr. 3	P 6	38
Kincora Gro. 3	P 6	38
Kincora Pk. 3	P 6	38
Kincora Rd. 3	P 6	38
King St. N. 7	J 8	43
King St. S. 2	K 9	43
Kingram La. 2	L10	44
Kings Av. 1	M 7	36
Kings Hospital School 8	H 8	42
Kings Inns St. 1	K 8	43
Kingsbridge 8	H 8	42
Kingsland Par. 8	K11	49
Kingsland Park Av. 8	K10	43
Kinvara Av. 7	F 5	33
Kinvara Dr. 7	E 5	33
Kinvara Gro. 7	E 5	33
Kinvara Pk. 7	E 5	33
Kinvara Rd. 7	E 5	33
Kippure Av. 12	C14	52
Kippure Pk. 11	F 4	21
Kirkwood 4	O11	51
Kirwan St. 7	H 8	42
Kirwan Street Cotts. 7	H 8	42
Kirwan St.		
Kitestown Rd., Howth	BB4	31
Knapton Rd., D.L.	U16	60
Knockcullen Lawn 14	F16	53
Knockcullen Dr.		
Knockcullen Pk. 14	F16	53
Knocklyon Dr.		
Knocklyon Av. 14	E16	53
Knocklyon Dr. 14	F16	53
Knocklyon Pk. 14	E16	53
Knocknarea Av. 12	F11	47
Knocknarea Rd. 12	E11	47
Knocknashee 14	N16	57
Kyle-Clare Rd. 4	O 9	45
Kylemore Av. 10	C10	40
Kylemore Dr. 10	C10	40
Kylemore Pk. N. 10	C10	40
Kylemore Pk. S. 10	C10	40
Kylemore Pk. W. 10	C10	40
Kylemore Rd. 10	C 9	40
La Touche Dr. 12	D10	40
La Touche Rd. 12	D11	46
La Vista Av., Howth	Y 4	30
Laburnum Rd. 14	M13	50
Lad La. 2	L10	44
Lagan Rd. 11	G 4	22
Lakelands Pk. 6	H14	54
Lally Rd. 10	D 9	40
Lambay Rd. 9	K 4	23
Lambs Ct. 8	H 9	42
Jamess St.		
Landen Rd. 10	C10	40
Landscape Av. 14	K15	55
Landscape Cres. 14	K15	55
Landscape Gdns. 14	K15	55
Landscape Pk. 14	K15	55
Landscape Rd. 14	K14	55
Lanesville, D.L.	T17	60
Langrishe Pl. 1	L 7	36
Summer Hill		
Lansdowne Gdns. 4	N10	45
Shelbourne Rd.		
Lansdowne La. 4	N10	45
Lansdowne Pk. 4	M10	44
Lansdowne Rd. 4	M10	44
Lansdowne Road Station 4	N10	45
Lansdowne Ter. 4	N11	51
Serpentine Av.		
Lansdowne Valley Rd. 12	D11	46
Lansdowne Village 4	N10	45
Laracor Gdns. 5	S 2	27
Laragh Clo. 5	S 2	27
Laragh Gro. 5	S 2	27
Laragh Clo.		
Larch Gro. 6	L12	50
Larchfield 14	L15	56
Larchfield Pk. 14	M15	56
Larchfield Rd. 14	M15	56
Larkfield Av. 6	H12	48
Larkfield Gdns. 6	H12	48
Larkfield Gro. 6	H12	48
Larkfield Pk. 6	H12	48
Larkhill Rd. 9	L 3	24
Laurel Av. 14	L16	56
Laurel Dr. 14	L16	56
Laurel Hill, D.L.	U17	60
Laurel Rd. 14	L16	56
Laurels, The 6	H13	48
Laurels, The 14	L16	56
Lavarna Gro. 6	G14	54
Lavarna Rd. 6	G13	48
Lavista Av., Killester 5	P 5	38
Lawn, The 11	G 3	22
Lawrence Gro. 3	O 6	37
Le Bas Ter. 6	J12	48
Leinster Rd. W.		
Le Vere Ter. 6	J11	49
Lea Cres. 4	O11	51
Lea Rd. 4	O11	51
Leahys Ter. 4	O10	45
Lee Rd. 11	H 5	34
Leeson Clo. 2	L10	44
Leeson La. 2	L10	44
Leeson Park Av. 6	L11	50
Leeson Pk. 6	L11	50
Leeson St. Lwr. 2	L10	44
Leeson St. Upr. 4	L11	50
Leeson Village 6	L11	50
Leicester Av. 6	J12	49
Leighlin Rd. 12	G12	48
Lein Gdns. 5	Q 4	26
(Gardini Lein)		
Lein Pk. 5	Q 3	26
Lein Rd. 5	Q 3	26
Leinster Av. 3	M 7	36
Leinster La. 2	L 9	44
Leinster St. S.		
Leinster Market 2	K 8	43
D'Olier St.		
Leinster Pl. 6	J12	49
Leinster Rd. 6	J12	49
Leinster Rd. W. 6	J12	49
Leinster Sq. 6	K12	49
Leinster St. 2	L 9	44
Leinster St. E. 3	M 7	36
Leinster St. N. 7	J 6	35
Leinster St. S. 2	L 9	44
Leix Rd. 7	H 6	34
Leland Pl. 1	M 8	44
Commons St.		
Lemon St. 2	K 9	43
Lennox Pl. 8	K11	49
Lennox St. 8	K11	49
Lentisk Lawn 5	S 2	27
Leo Av. 7	K 7	35
Leo St.		
Leo St. 7	K 7	35
Leslies Buildings 7	J 7	35
Leukos Rd. 4	O 9	45
Liberty La. 8	K10	43
Library Rd., D.L.	U16	60
Liffey St. 10	E 9	41
Liffey St. Lwr. 1	K 8	43
Liffey St. Upr. 1	K 8	43
Liffey St. W. 7	H 8	42
Benburb St.		
Liffey Tunnel	N 9	45
Lime St. 2	M 9	44
Limekiln Clo. 12	E14	53
Limekiln Dr. 12	E14	53
Limekiln Gro. 12	E13	47
Limekiln La. 12	E14	53
Limekiln Pk. 12	E14	53
Limekiln Rd. 12	D14	52
Limewood Av. 5	R 2	27
Limewood Pk. 5	R 2	27
Limewood Rd. 5	R 2	27
Lincoln La. 7	J 8	43
Lincoln Pl. 2	L 9	44
Linden Gro., Stillorgan	Q16	58
Lindsay Rd. 9	J 6	35
Linenhall Par. 7	J 8	43
Linenhall Ter. 7	J 8	43
Link Rd., D.L.	W17	61
Lisburn St. 7	J 8	43
Liscannor Rd. 7	G 5	34
Lisle Rd. 12	E12	47
Lismore Rd. 12	G12	48
Lissadel Av. 12	F11	47
Lissadel Clo. 12	F11	47
Lissadel Dr. 12	F11	47
Lissadel Pk. 12	F11	47
Lissadel Rd. 12	F11	47
Litten La. 1	K 8	43
Little Britain St. 7	J 8	43
Little Longford St. 2	K 9	43
Loftus La. 1	K 8	43
Lombard Ct. 2	L 9	44
Lombard St. E. 2	L 9	44
Lombard St. W. 8	J10	43
Lomond Av. 3	M 6	36
Londonbridge Rd. 4	N10	45
Long La. 7	K 7	35
Long La., Tenter Fields 8	J10	43
Long Mile Rd. 10	C12	46
Longford La. 8	K 9	43
Longford St. Gt.		
Longford Pl., D.L.	U16	60
Longford St. Gt. 8	K 9	43
Longford St. Lit. 2	K10	43
Digges St.		
Longford Ter., D.L.	T16	60
Longs Pl. 8	H 9	42
Longwood Av. 8	J11	49
Longwood Pk. 14	J16	55
Lorcan Av. 9	M 2	24
Lorcan Cres. 9	M 2	24
Lorcan Dr. 9	M 2	24
Lorcan Gro. 9	M 2	24
Lorcan O'Toole Pk. 12	F13	47
Lorcan Pk. 9	M 2	24
Lorcan Rd. 9	M 2	24
Lorcan Vill. 9	N 2	25
Lord Edward St. 2	K 9	43
Loreto Av. 14	J16	55
Loreto Cres. 14	J16	55
Loreto Pk. 14	J16	55
Loreto Rd. 8	H10	42
Loreto Row 14	J16	55
Loreto Ter. 14	J16	55
Lorgan Grn. 9	N 2	25
Lorne Ter. 8	G 9	42
Brookfield Rd.		
Lotts 1	K 8	43
Lough Derg Rd. 5	R 4	27
Lourdes Rd. 8	H10	42
Louvain 14	N15	57
Louvain Glade 14	N15	57
Love La. E. 2	M10	44
Lower Churchtown Rd. 14	L14	56
Lower Dodder Rd. 14	H14	54
Luby Rd. 8	F 9	41
Lugnaquilla Av. 12	C14	52
Luke St. 2	L 8	44
Lullymore Ter. 8	H11	48
Lurgan St. 7	J 8	43
Lynchs La. 10	C 9	40
Lynchs Pl. 7	J 7	35
Mabbot La. 1	L 8	44
Mabel St. 3	L 6	36
Macken St. 2	M 9	44
Madeleine Ter. 8	E 9	41
Madison Rd. 8	G10	42
Magennis Pl. 2	L 9	44
Magenta Cres. 9	M 2	24
Magenta Hall 9	M 2	24
Magenta Pl., D.L.	V17	61
Mageough Home 6	L13	50
Maginesss Sq. 2	L 9	44
Pearse St.		
Mahers Pl. 2	M 9	44
Macken St.		
Maiden Row, Chapelizod	C 8	40
Main Rd. 8	C 5	32
Main St. 5	R 4	27
Main St., Blackrock	R15	59
Main St., Dundrum 14	L16	56
Main St., Finglas 11	G 3	22
Main St., Howth	BB3	31
Main St., Rathfarnham 14	H15	54
Malachi Rd. 7	H 8	42

Name	Grid
Malahide Rd. 3	N 6 37
Malahide Rd. 5	O 4 25
Mallin Av. 8	H10 42
Mallin Gdns., D.L.	V16 61
Malone Gdns. 4	N10 45
Malpas Pl. 8	J10 43
Malpas St.	
Malpas St. 8	J10 43
Malpas Ter. 8	J10 43
Malpas St.	
Manders Ter. 6	L11 50
Mangerton Rd. 12	E11 47
Mannix Rd. 3	K 5 35
Manor Pl. 7	H 8 42
Manor St. 7	H 8 42
Mansion House 2	L 9 44
Maolbuille Rd. 11	K 3 23
Maple Rd. 14	M13 50
Maples, The, D.L.	T16 60
Maquay Bridge	M10 44
Maretimo Gdns. E., D.L.	S15 59
Maretimo Gdns. W., D.L.	S15 59
Newtown Av.	
Maretimo Rd., D.L.	S15 59
Maretimo Vill., D.L.	S15 59
Margaret Pl. 4	N10 45
Marguerite Rd. 9	K 5 35
Marian Cres. 14	G16 54
Marian Dr. 14	G15 54
Marian Gro. 14	H16 54
Marian Pk., Baldoyle	U 2 28
Marian Pk., Rathfarnham 14	G16 54
Marian Rd. 14	G16 54
Marine Av., D.L.	W17 61
Marine Ct., D.L.	W17 61
Marine Dr. 4	O10 45
Marine Par., D.L.	W17 61
Marine Rd., D.L.	V16 61
Marine Ter., D.L.	V16 61
Marino Av. 3	N 6 37
Marino Cres. 3	N 6 37
Marino Grn. 3	N 6 37
Marino Mart 3	N 6 37
Marino Park Av. 3	N 6 37
Marino Pk. 3	M 6 36
Marion Vill. 8	H10 42
Cork St.	
Mark St. 2	L 9 44
Market St. S. 8	H 9 42
Marks Alley W. 8	J 9 43
Marks La. 2	L 9 44
Marlborough Pl. 1	L 8 44
Marlborough Rd. 7	G 7 34
Marlborough Rd., Donnybrook 4	L12 50
Marlborough St. 1	K 8 43
Marne Vill. 7	J 7 35
Marrowbone La. 8	H10 42
Marshalsea La. 8	H 9 42
Martello Av., D.L.	V16 61
Martello Ter., D.L.	Q14 58
Martin Savage Pk., Ashtown	D 5 32
Martin Savage Rd. 7	E 6 33
Martin St. 8	K11 49
Martins Row, Chapelizod	C 8 40
Mary St. 1	K 8 43
Mary St. Lit. 7	K 8 43
Maryfield Av. 5	O 3 25
Maryfield Cres. 5	O 3 25
Maryfield Dr. 5	O 3 25
Marys Abbey 7	K 8 43
Marys La. 7	J 8 43
Maryville Rd. 5	Q 4 26
Mask Av. 5	P 3 26
Mask Cres. 5	P 3 26
Mask Dr. 5	P 3 26
Mask Grn. 5	P 3 26
Mask Rd. 5	P 3 26
Masonic School 4	N11 51
Mastersons La. 2	K10 43
Charlemont St.	
Mater Misericordiae Hospital 7	K 7 35
Mather Rd. N., Stillorgan	O15 57
Mather Rd. S., Stillorgan	O15 57
Matt Talbot Ct. 1	L 7 36
Maunsel Pl. 7	K 7 35
Mountjoy St.	
Maxwell Rd. 6	K12 49
Maxwell St. 8	H10 42
May La. 7	J 8 43
May St. 3	L 6 36
Mayfield Rd., Kilmainham 8	G10 42
Mayfield Rd., Terenure 6	H13 48
Mayola Ct. 14	L15 56
Mayor St. Lwr. 1	M 8 44
Mayor St. Upr. 1	M 8 44
Maywood Av. 5	S 4 27
Maywood Clo. 5	S 4 27
Maywood Cres. 5	S 4 27
Maywood Dr. 5	S 4 27
Maywood Gro. 5	S 4 27
Maywood La. 5	S 4 27
Maywood Pk. 5	S 4 27
Maywood Rd. 5	S 4 27
McAuley Av. 5	Q 3 26
(Ascal Mac Amhlaoi)	
McAuley Dr. 5	Q 3 26
McAuley Pk. 5	Q 4 26
McAuley Rd. 5	Q 3 26
McCabe Vill., Booterstown	P14 58
McCanns La. 1	K 8 43
Denmark St.	
McCarthys Bldgs. 7	J 6 35
Cabra Rd.	
McDowell Av. 8	G 9 42
McKee Av. 11	G 2 22
McKee Barracks 7	G 7 34
McKee Dr. 7	G 7 34
McKee Pk. 7	G 7 34
McKee Rd. 11	H 2 22
McMahon St. 8	J10 43
McMorrough 6	J13 49
Meades Ter. 2	M 9 44
Meadow Pk. 14	K16 55
Meadows, The 5	Q 4 26
Meath Hospital 8	J10 43
Meath Pl. 8	J 9 43
Meath Sq. 8	J 9 43
Meath St.	
Meath St. 8	J 9 43
Meetinghouse La. 7	K 8 43
Abbey Mabbey	
Mellifont Av., D.L.	V16 61
Mellowes Av. 11	F 2 21
Mellowes Pk. 11	F 2 21
Mellowes Rd. 11	F 2 21
Melrose Av. 3	M 6 36
Melvin Rd. 6	H13 48
Memorial Rd. 1	L 8 44
Mercer St. Lwr. 2	K 9 43
Mercer St. Upr. 2	K10 43
Mercers Hospital 2	K 9 43
Merchamp 3	Q 6 38
Merchants Quay 8	J 9 43
Merchants Rd. 3	N 8 45
Merlyn Dr. 4	O12 51
Merlyn Pk. 4	O12 51
Merlyn Rd. 4	O12 51
Merrion Pl. 2	L 9 44
Merrion Rd. 4	N11 51
Merrion Row 2	L10 44
Merrion Sq. E. 2	L 9 44
Merrion Sq. N. 2	L 9 44
Merrion Sq. S. 2	L 9 44
Merrion Sq. W. 2	L 9 44
Merrion St. Lwr. 2	L 9 44
Clare St.	
Merrion St. Upr. 2	L10 44
Merrion View Av. 4	O12 51
Merton Av. 8	H10 42
Merton Dr. 6	L12 50
Merton Rd. 6	L13 50
Merville Av., Fairview 3	M 6 36
Mespil Rd. 4	L10 44
Middle Third 5	P 5 38
Military Cemetery 7	G 6 34
Military Rd., Kilmainham 8	G 9 42
Military Rd., Rathmines 6	K11 49
Mill La. 8	J10 43
New Market	
Mill La., Ashtown	D 5 32
Mill La., Santry 9	J10 43
Millbourne Av. 9	K 5 35
Millbrook Av. 5	R 2 27
Millbrook Dr. 5	R 2 27
Millbrook Gro. 5	R 2 27
Millbrook Lawn 14	H16 54
Millbrook Pk. 5	R 3 27
Millbrook Rd. 5	R 2 27
Millbrook Vill. 5	R 2 27
Millgate Dr. 12	E14 53
Millmount Av. 9	K 5 35
Millmount Pl. 9	L 5 36
Millmount Ter. 9	L 5 36
Drumcondra	
Millmount Vill. 9	K 5 35
Millrown Bridge Rd. 14	M13 50
Milltown Dr. 14	K15 55
Milltown Golf Course 14	L15 56
Milltown Gro. 14	K15 55
Milltown Path 6	L13 50
Milltown Rd. 6	L14 56
Misery Hill 2	M 9 44
Moatfield Av. 5	Q 3 26
Moatfield Pk. 5	Q 3 26
Moatfield Rd. 5	Q 2 26
Moeran Rd. 12	E12 47
Moira Rd. 7	H 8 42
Moland Pl. 1	L 8 44
Talbot St.	
Molesworth Pl. 2	L 9 44
Molesworth St.	
Molesworth St. 2	L 9 44
Molyneux Yd. 8	J 9 43
Monasterboice Rd. 12	G11 48
Monck Pl. 7	J 7 35
Monkstown and Seapoint Station, D.L.	S15 59
Monkstown Av., D.L.	T17 60
Monkstown Cres., D.L.	T16 60
Monkstown Farm, D.L.	T17 60
Monkstown Gro., D.L.	T17 60
Monkstown Rd., D.L.	S15 59
Montague La. 2	K10 43
Montague St. 2	K10 43
Montpelier Dr. 7	H 8 42
Montpelier Gdns. 7	G 8 42
Montpelier Hill 7	H 8 42
Montpelier Par., D.L.	S16 59
Montpelier Pl., D.L.	S15 59
Montrose Av. 5	N 3 25
Montrose Clo. 5	N 3 25
Montrose Cres. 5	O 3 25
Montrose Dr. 5	N 3 25
Montrose Gro. 5	N 3 25
Montrose Pk. 5	N 3 25
Moore La. 1	K 8 43
Moore St. 1	K 8 43
Morehampton La. 4	M11 50
Morehampton Rd. 4	M11 50
Morehampton Ter. 4	M11 50
Morgan Pl. 7	J 9 43
Inns Quay	
Morning Star Av. 7	J 8 43
Brunswick St. N.	
Morning Star Rd. 8	H10 42
Mornington Rd. 6	L12 50
Morrogh Ter. 3	M 5 36
Moss St. 2	L 8 44
Mount Albion Ter. 14	L16 56
Mount Annville Convent 14	O16 57
Mount Annville Lawn 14	N16 57
Mount Annville Rd. 14	N16 57
Mount Anville, Stillorgan	O16 57
Mount Argus Gro. 6	H12 48
Mount Argus Rd. 6	H12 48
Mount Brown 8	G 9 42
Mount Carmel Av. 14	M15 56
Mount Carmel Convent 14	N14 57
Mount Carmel Pk., Firhouse	D16 52
Mount Carmel Rd. 14	M15 56
Mount Dillon Ct. 5	P 3 26
Mount Drummond Av. 6	J11 49
Mount Drummond Sq. 6	J11 49
Mount Eden Rd. 4	M12 50
Mount Harold Ter. 6	J12 49
Mount Jerome Cemetery 6	H11 48
Mount Merrion Av., D.L.	P15 58
Mount Olive Gro. 5	S 2 27
Mount Olive Pk. 5	S 2 27
Mount Olive Rd. 5	S 2 27
Mount Prospect Av. 3	Q 6 38
Mount Prospect Dr. 3	Q 5 38
Mount Prospect Gro. 3	R 6 39
Mount Prospect Pk. 3	Q 6 38
Mount Shannon Rd. 8	G10 42
Mount St. Lwr. 2	M 9 44
Mount St. Upr. 2	L10 44
Mount Street Cres. 2	M10 44
Mount Tallant Av.	H13 48
Mount Tallant Ter. 6	H13 48
Harolds Cross Rd.	
Mount Temple Rd. 7	H 8 42
Mount Town Lwr., D.L.	U17 60
Mount Town Pk., D.L.	U17 60
Mount Town Upr., D.L.	T16 60
Mount Wood, D.L.	U17 60
Mountain View Av. 6	J12 49
Harolds Cross Rd.	
Mountain View Rd. 6	L12 50
Mountainview Pk. 14	K16 55
Mountdown Dr. 12	E14 53
Mountdown Pk. 12	E14 53
Mountdown Rd. 12	E14 53
Mountjoy Cotts. 7	K 6 35
Mountjoy Pl. 1	L 7 36
Mountjoy Prison 7	K 6 35
Mountjoy Prison Cotts. 7	K 6 35
Cowley Pl.	
Mountjoy Sq. E. 1	L 7 36
Mountjoy Sq. N. 1	K 7 35
Mountjoy Sq. S. 1	L 7 36
Mountjoy Sq. W. 1	K 7 35
Mountjoy St. 7	K 7 35
Mountjoy St. Mid. 7	J 7 35
Mountpleasant Av. Lwr. 6	K11 49
Mountpleasant Av. Upr. 6	K11 49
Mountpleasant Bldgs. 6	K11 49
Mountpleasant Par. 6	K11 49
Mountpleasant Pl.	
Mountpleasant Pl. 6	K11 49
Mountpleasant Sq. 6	K11 49
Mourne Rd. 12	E11 47
Moy Elta Rd. 3	M 7 36
Moyclare Clo., Baldoyle	V 2 29
Moyclare Pk., Baldoyle	V 2 29

Street	Grid
Moyclare Rd., Baldoyle	V 2 29
Moyle Rd. 11	G 5 34
Moyne Rd. 6	L12 50
Muckross Av. 12	E13 47
Muckross Cres. 12	E13 47
Muckross Dr. 12	F13 47
Muckross Grn. 12	F13 47
Muckross Gro. 12	E13 47
Muckross Par. 7	K 6 35
Killarney Par.	
Muckross Pk. 12	F13 47
Mulgrave St., D.L.	V16 61
Mulgrave Ter., D.L.	V16 61
Mulroy Rd. 7	H 6 34
Mulvey Pk. 14	M15 56
Munster St. 7	J 6 35
Murrays Cotts. 10	E 9 41
Sarsfield Rd.	
Murtagh Rd. 7	H 8 42
Muskerry Rd. 10	C 9 40
Myra Cotts. 8	F 9 41
Myrtle Av., D.L.	V17 61
Myrtle Pk., D.L.	V17 61
Nanikin Av. 5	R 4 27
Nash St. 8	D10 40
Nashville Pk., Howth	BB3 31
Nashville Rd., Howth	BB3 31
Nassau Pl. 2	L 9 44
Nassau St. 2	K 9 43
National Maternity Hospital 2	M 9 44
National Museum 2	L 9 44
Navan Rd., Castleknock	C 4 20
Neagh Rd. 6	H13 48
Nelson St. 7	K 7 35
Nephin Rd. 7	F 6 33
Neville Rd. 6	K13 49
New Ireland Rd. 8	G10 42
New Lisburn St. 7	J 8 43
Coleraine Rd.	
New Rd., Howth	BB4 31
New Rd., Inchicore	D10 40
New Row S. 8	J10 43
New St. S. 8	J10 43
New Wapping St. 1	M 8 44
Newbridge Av. 4	N10 45
Newbridge Dr. 4	N10 45
Newbrook Av. 5	T 2 28
Newbrook Rd. 5	T 2 28
Newcomen Av. 3	M 7 36
Newcomen Bridge	M 7 36
Newcomen Ct. 3	M 7 36
North Strand Rd.	
Newgrange Rd. 7	H 6 34
Newgrove Av. 4	O10 45
Newmarket 8	J10 43
Newport St. 8	H 9 42
Newtown Av., D.L.	R15 59
Newtown Cotts. 5	Q 2 26
Newtown Dr. 5	Q 2 26
Newtown Pk., Tallaght	C16 52
Newtown Vill., D.L.	S15 59
Newtownsmith, D.L.	W16 61
Niall St. 7	H 7 34
Nicholas Av. 7	J 8 43
Church St. Old	
Nicholas Pl. 8	J 9 43
Patrick St.	
Nicholas St. 8	J 9 43
Nore Rd. 11	G 5 34
Norfolk Market 1	K 8 43
Parnell St.	
Norfolk Rd. 7	J 6 35
Norseman Pl. 7	H 8 42
North Av., Stillorgan	O15 57
North Branch Rd. N. 21	P 8 62
Alexandra Rd.	
North Circular Rd. 7	G 8 42
North Great Georges St. 1	K 7 35
North Rd. No.1 1	O 8 45
Alexandra Rd.	
North Strand Rd. 1	M 7 36
North Wall Extension 1	N 9 45
North Wall Quay 1	M 8 44
North Wall Station 1	M 8 44
Northbrook Av. Lwr. 1	M 7 36
North Strand Rd.	
Northbrook Av. Upr. 3	M 7 36
Northbrook Rd. 6	L11 50
Northbrook Ter. 3	M 7 36
Northbrook Vill. 6	L11 50
Northbrook Rd.	
Northcote Av., D.L.	U16 60
Northcourt Av. Lwr. 3	M 7 36
Northland Dr. 11	J 4 23
Northland Gro. 11	H 4 22
Northumberland Av., D.L.	V16 61
Northumberland Pl., D.L.	V16 61
Northumberland Rd.	
Northumberland Rd. 4	M10 45
Northumberland Sq. 1	L 8 44
Nortons Av. 7	J 7 35
Norwood Pk. 6	M12 50
Nottingham St. 3	M 7 36
Nowlan Av. 14	L16 56
Nugent Rd. 14	K15 55
Nutgrove Av. 14	J16 55
(Ascal An Charrain Chno)	
Nutgrove Pk. 14	M14 56
Nutley Av. 4	O12 51
Nutley La. 4	O13 51
Nutley Pk. 4	O13 51
Nutley Rd. 4	N12 51
O'Brien Rd. 12	E12 47
O'Briens Institute 3	N 5 37
O'Briens Place N. 9	K 5 35
O'Briens Ter. 9	J 6 35
Prospect Rd.	
O'Carolan Rd. 8	J10 43
O'Connell Av. 7	J 7 35
O'Connell Gdns. 4	N10 45
O'Connell St. Lwr. 1	K 8 43
O'Connell St. Upr. 1	K 8 43
O'Curry Av. 8	J10 43
O'Curry Rd. 8	J10 43
O'Daly Rd. 9	K 5 35
O'Devaney Gdns. 7	G 8 42
O'Donnell Gdns., D.L.	V17 61
O'Donnovan Rossa Bridge	J 9 43
O'Donoghue St. 8	E10 41
O'Donovan Rd. 8	J10 43
O'Dwyer Rd. 12	E12 47
O'Hogan Rd. 10	D 9 40
O'Leary Rd. 8	F10 41
O'Moore Rd. 10	D 9 40
O'Neachtain Rd. 9	K 5 35
O'Neills Bldgs. 8	K10 43
O'Quinn Av. 8	G 9 42
O'Rahilly Par. 1	K 8 43
Moore St.	
O'Reillys Av. 8	G 9 42
O'Sullivan Av. 3	M 7 36
Oak Park Av. 9	M 2 24
Oak Park Clo. 9	M 2 24
Oak Park Dr. 9	M 2 24
Oak Park Gro. 9	M 2 24
Oak Rd. 9	N 5 37
Oakdown Rd. 14	K16 55
Oakfield Pl. 8	J10 43
Oaklands Cres. 6	K13 49
Oaklands Dr. 4	N11 51
Oaklands Dr. 6	J13 49
Oaklands Pk. 4	N11 51
Oaklands Ter. 4	N11 51
Serpentine Av.	
Oaklands Ter. 6	J13 49
Oaklawn, D.L.	S16 59
Oakley Gro., D.L.	R16 59
Oakley Pk. 3	Q 6 38
Oakley Pk., Stillorgan	R16 59
Oakley Rd. 6	L12 50
Oaks, The 14	L16 56
Oakwood Av. 11	H 2 22
Oakwood Pk. 11	H 2 22
Observatory La. 6	K11 49
Rathmines Rd.	
Ocean Pier 1	O 8 45
Offaly Rd. 7	H 6 34
Offington Av., Howth	Y 3 30
Offington Ct., Howth	Y 3 30
Offington Dr., Howth	Y 3 30
Offington Lawn, Howth	Y 3 30
Olaf Rd. 7	H 8 42
Old Bridge Rd. 14	F15 53
Old Cabra Rd. 7	G 6 34
Old Camden St. 2	K10 43
Old County Rd. 12	F11 47
Old Dunleary, D.L.	U16 60
Old Kilmainham 8	G 9 42
Old Mountpleasant 6	K11 49
Old Naas Rd. 12	C11 46
Old Rectory Pk. 14	M16 56
Oldtown Av. 9	K 2 23
Oldtown Pk. 9	K 2 23
Oldtown Rd. 9	L 2 24
Olivemount Gro. 14	M14 56
Olivemount Rd. 14	M14 56
Oliver Bond St. 8	J 9 43
Oliver Plunkett Av., Irishtown 4	N 9 45
Oliver Plunkett Av., D.L.	T17 60
Oliver Plunkett Cres., D.L.	T17 60
Oliver Plunkett Av.	
Oliver Plunkett Rd., D.L.	T17 60
Oliver Plunkett Ter., D.L.	T17 60
Oliver Plunkett Vill., D.L.	T17 60
Olney Cres. 6	H14 54
Ontario Ter. 6	K11 49
Ophaly Ct. 14	M15 56
Orchard La., D.L.	R16 59
Orchard Rd. 5	T 4 28
Orchard Rd. 3	K13 49
Orchard, The, 5	P 5 38
Orchardston 14	H16 54
Orchardstown Av. 14	G16 54
Orchardstown Dr. 14	F16 53
Orchardstown Pk. 14	G16 54
Orchardstown Vill. 14	G16 54
Ordnance Survey Office	C 6 32
Oriel St. Lwr. 1	M 8 44
Oriel St. Upr. 1	M 8 44
Ormeau St. 4	N 9 45
Ormond Market Sq. 7	J 9 43
Ormond Quay Upr.	
Ormond Quay Lwr. 1	K 8 43
Ormond Quay Upr. 7	J 9 43
Ormond Rd. 9	L 5 36
Ormond Rd. N. 9	L 5 36
Ormond Rd. S., Rathmines 6	K12 49
Ormond Sq. 7	J 8 43
Ormond St. 8	J10 43
Orwell Gdns. 14	K14 55
Orwell Park Av. 12	E15 53
Orwell Park Clo. 12	E15 53
Orwell Park Cres. 12	F15 53
Orwell Park Dr. 12	F15 53
Orwell Park Glade 12	F15 53
Orwell Park Glen 12	E15 53
Orwell Park Grn. 12	E15 53
Orwell Park Lawns 12	E15 53
Orwell Park Way 12	E15 53
Orwell Rd. 6	K14 55
Orwell Rd. 6	J13 49
Orwell Woods 6	K14 55
Oscar Sq. 8	J10 43
Osprey Av., Tallaght	E14 53
Osprey Lawn, Tallaght	E14 53
Osprey Pk., Tallaght	D14 52
Osprey Rd., Tallaght	E15 53
Ossory Rd. 3	M 7 36
Ossory Sq. 8	J10 43
Ostman Pl. 7	H 8 42
Oswald Rd. 4	O10 45
Otranto Pl., D.L.	V17 61
Oulton Rd. 3	P 6 38
Our Ladys Hospice 6	J11 49
Our Ladys Hospital 12	E11 47
Our Ladys Rd. 8	H10 42
Ovoca Rd. 8	J10 43
Owendoher Av. 14	H15 54
Owendoher Cres. 14	H15 54
Owendore Av. 14	H15 54
Owendore Cres. 14	H15 54
Owens Av. 8	G 9 42
Owenstown Pk., Stillorgan	O15 57
Oxford Rd. 6	K11 49
Oxford Ter. 3	M 8 44
Church Rd.	
Oxford Ter. 6	K11 49
Oxford Rd.	
Oxmantown La. 7	H 8 42
Blackhall Pl.	
Oxmantown Rd. 7	H 7 34
Oxmantown Rd. Lwr. 7	H 8 42
Arbour Hill	
Pacelli Av., Baldoyle	U 3 28
Paddock, The 7	D 5 32
Pairc Baile Munna 11	J 3 23
Pakenham Rd., D.L.	T16 60
Palace St. 2	K 9 43
Dame St.	
Palmerston Gdns. 6	K13 49
Palmerston La. 6	L13 50
Palmerston Pk. 6	K13 49
Palmerston Pl. 7	J 7 35
Palmerston Rd. 6	K12 49
Palmerston Vill. 6	K13 49
Palms, The, 14	N15 57
Paradise Pl. 7	K 7 35
Park Av. 4	O11 51
Park Cres. 8	F 6 33
Park Dr. 6	L12 50
Park La. 4	O11 51
Park La. E. 2	L 9 44
Lincoln Pl.	
Park La., Chapelizod	C 8 40
Park Lawn 3	R 5 39
Park Pl. 8	F 9 41
Islandbridge	
Park Rd. 7	E 5 33
Park Rd., D.L.	V16 61
Park St. 10	E 9 41
Park Ter. 8	J 9 43
Park View Av. 6	K12 49
Rathmines Rd.	
Park View, Castleknock	C 5 32
Parkgate St. 8	H 8 42
Parkmore Dr. 6	G14 54
Parkview Av. 6	J12 49
Parliament Row 2	K 9 43
Fleet St.	
Parliament St. 2	K 9 43
Parnell Av. 12	J11 49
Parnell Pl. 1	K 7 35
Parnell Rd. 12	H10 42
Parnell Sq. E. 1	K 7 35

Street	Grid
Parnell Sq. N. 1	K 7 35
Parnell Sq. W. 1	K 8 43
Parnell St. 1	K 8 43
Partridge Ter. 8	D10 40
Patrician Pk., D.L.	T17 60
Patrician Vill., Stillorgan	Q16 58
Patrick Doyle Rd. 14	L14 56
Patrick St. 8	J 9 43
Patrick St., D.L.	U16 60
Patricks Clo. S. 8	J 9 43
Patrickswell Pl. 11	G 3 22
Patriotic Ter. 8	G 9 42
Brookfield Rd.	
Pearse House 2	L 9 44
Pearse Sq. E. 2	M 9 44
Pearse Sq. N. 2	M 9 44
Pearse Sq. W. 2	M 9 44
Pearse St. 2	L 9 44
Pearse Station 2	L 9 44
Pembroke Cotts., Dundrum 14	M16 56
Pembroke Cotts., Donnybrook 4	M12 50
Pembroke Cotts., Ringsend 4	N 9 45
Pembroke Cotts., D.L.	P14 58
Pembroke Gdns. 4	M10 44
Pembroke La. 2	L10 44
Pembroke La. 4	M10 44
Pembroke Pk. 4	M11 50
Pembroke Pl. 4	N11 51
Herbert Pk.	
Pembroke Rd. 4	M10 44
Pembroke Row 2	L10 44
Pembroke St. 4	N 9 45
Pembroke St. Lwr. 2	L10 44
Pembroke St. Upr. 2	L10 44
Penrose Str. 4	N 9 45
Percy French Rd. 12	E12 47
Percy La. 4	M10 44
Percy Pl. 4	M10 44
Peter Row 8	K 9 43
Peter St. 8	K 9 43
Peters Pl. 2	K10 43
Petersons Ct. 2	L 8 44
Petrie Rd. 8	J10 43
Phibsborough 7	J 7 35
Phibsborough Av. 7	J 7 35
Phibsborough Pl. 7	J 7 35
Phibsborough Rd. 7	J 7 35
Philipsburgh Av. 3	M 6 36
Philipsburgh Ter. 3	M 6 36
Philomena Ter. 4	N 9 45
Phoenix St. 10	E 9 41
Phoenix St. 7	J 8 43
Pigeon House Rd. 4	O 9 45
Piles Bldgs. 8	K 9 43
Golden La.	
Piles Ter. 8	L 9 44
Pim St. 8	H 9 42
Pimlico 8	J 9 43
Pimlico Sq. 8	J 9 43
The Coombe	
Pine Rd. 4	O 9 45
Pinebrook Av. 5	O 4 25
Pinebrook Cres. 5	O 4 25
Pinebrook Av.	
Pinebrook Gro. 5	O 4 25
Pinebrook Rd.	
Pinebrook Rd. 5	O 4 25
Pinebrook Ri. 5	O 4 25
Pinewood Av. 11	J 2 23
Pinewood Cres. 11	J 2 23
Pinewood Dr. 11	J 2 23
Pinewood Grn. 11	J 2 23
Pinewood Gro. 11	J 2 23
Pinewood Pk. 14	H16 54
Pinewood Vill. 11	J 2 23
Pleasants La. 8	K10 43
Pleasants Pl. 8	K10 43
Pleasants St. 8	K10 43
Plunkett Grn. 11	F 2 21
Plunkett Rd. 11	F 2 21
Poddle Pk. 12	G13 48
Poolbeg St. 2	L 8 44
Poole St. 8	J 9 43
Poplar Row 3	M 6 36
Poplars, The, D.L.	T16 60
Portland Clo. 1	L 7 36
Portland Pl. 1	K 6 35
Portland Row 1	L 7 36
Portland Row N. 1	L 7 36
Portland St. 8	H 9 42
Portland St. N. 1	L 7 36
Portmahon St. 8	G10 42
Portobello Barracks 6	J11 49
Portobello Harbour 8	K11 49
Portobello Pl. 8	K11 49
Portobello Harbour	
Portobello Rd. 8	J11 49
Portobello Pl. 8	J11 49
Clanbrassil St. Upr.	
Potato Market 7	J 8 43
Green St. Lit.	
Potters Alley 1	L 8 44
Powers Ct. 2	M10 44
Powers Sq. 8	J 9 43
Dillon St.	
Prebend St. 7	J 8 43
Preistfield Ter. 8	H10 42
South Circular Rd.	
Preston St. 1	J 8 43
Prices La. 2	K 8 43
Prices La. 6	K11 49
Priestfield Cotts. 8	H10 42
Priestfield Dr. 8	H10 42
South Circular Rd.	
Primrose Av. 7	J 7 35
Primrose St. 7	J 7 35
Prince Arthur Ter. 6	K12 49
Prince of Wales Ter. 4	N11 51
Princes St. N. 1	K 8 43
Princes St. S. 2	L 9 44
Princeton 14	N15 57
Priory Av., Stillorgan	Q15 58
Priory Dr., Stillorgan	P16 58
Priory Gro., Stillorgan	P16 58
Priory Rd. 6	H12 48
Proby Sq., D.L.	R16 59
Probys La. 1	K 8 43
Promenade Rd. 1	O 7 37
Prospect Av. 9	J 5 35
Prospect Cemetery 11	J 5 35
Prospect La. 6	M13 50
Prospect Rd. 9	J 6 35
Prospect Sq. 9	J 5 35
Prospect Ter., Sandymount 4	O10 45
Protestant Row 2	K10 43
Prussia St. 7	H 7 34
Purser Gdns. 6	K12 49
Quarry Cotts. 12	E13 47
Quarry Dr. 12	E13 47
Quarry Rd., Cabra 7	H 6 34
Queen Maev Bridge	H 9 42
Queen St. 7	J 8 43
Queens Pk., D.L.	S16 59
Queens Rd., D.L.	V16 61
Quinns La. 2	L10 44
Rafters La. 12	F11 47
Rafters Rd. 12	F11 47
Raglan La. 4	M11 50
Raglan Rd. 4	M11 50
Raheny Pk. 5	S 4 27
Raheny Rd. 5	R 3 27
Raheny Station	R 4 27
Railway Av. 8	E10 41
Tyrconnell Rd.	
Railway Av., Inchicore 8	D10 40
Railway Av., Sutton	W 2 29
Railway Cotts. 4	N11 51
Serpentine Av.	
Railway St. 1	L 8 44
Railway Ter. 2	M 9 44
Greenore Ter.	
Rainsford Av. 8	H 9 42
Rainsford St. 8	H 9 42
Raleigh Sq. 12	F11 47
Ramilies Rd. 10	C 9 40
Ramleh Clo. 6	M13 50
Ramleh Pk. 6	M13 50
Ramleh Vill. 6	M13 50
Ranelagh Av. 6	L11 50
Ranelagh Bridge	Y 3 30
Ranelagh Rd. 6	K11 49
Raphoe Rd. 12	F11 47
Rath Row 2	L 8 44
Rathdown Av. 6	H14 54
Rathdown Cres. 6	H14 54
Rathdown Dr. 6	H14 54
Rathdown Pk. 6	H14 54
Rathdown Rd. 7	J 7 35
Rathdown Vill. 6	H14 54
Rathdrum Rd. 12	H11 48
Rathfarnham Bridge	H15 54
Rathfarnham Castle 14	H15 54
Rathfarnham Demesne	J15 55
Rathfarnham Pk. 14	H14 54
Rathfarnham Rd. 14	H15 54
Rathfarnham Wd. 14	J15 55
Rathgar Av. 6	J12 49
Rathgar Rd. 6	J13 49
Rathland Dr. 12	G13 48
(Ceide Raitleann)	
Rathland Rd. 12	G13 48
Rathlin Rd. 9	K 4 23
Rathmines Av. 6	J12 49
Rathmines Castle 6	K12 49
Rathmines Rd. Lwr. 6	K12 49
Rathmines Rd. Upr. 6	K12 49
Rathmore Pk. 5	S 4 27
Rathvale Av. 5	Q 2 26
Rathvale Dr. 5	Q 2 26
Rathvale Gro. 5	Q 2 26
Rathvale Av.	
Rathvale Pk. 5	Q 2 26
Rathvilly Dr. 11	F 4 21
Rathvilly Pk. 11	F 3 21
Ratoath Av. 11	E 3 21
Ratoath Dr. 11	E 3 21
Ratoath Rd. 11	E 3 21
Ratra Rd. 7	E 6 33
Ravensdale Pk. 12	G13 48
Ravensdale Rd. 3	N 7 37
Raymond St. 8	J10 43
Red Cow La. 7	J 8 43
Redesdale Cres., Stillorgan	O16 57
Redesdale Rd., Stillorgan	O16 57
Redmonds Hill 2	K10 43
Redwood Ct. 14	K15 55
Reginald Sq. 8	J 9 43
Gray St.	
Reginald St. 8	J 9 43
Rehoboth Av. 8	H10 42
Rehoboth Pl. 8	H10 42
Restoration La. 2	L10 44
Reuben Av. 8	H10 42
Reuben St. 8	H10 42
Rialto Bldgs. 8	G10 42
Rialto Bridge	G10 42
Rialto Dr. 8	G10 42
Rialto St. 8	G10 42
Ribh Av. 5	Q 4 26
Ribh Rd. 5	Q 4 26
Richelieu Pk. 4	O12 51
Richmond Av. N. 3	M 6 36
Richmond Av. S. 6	L13 50
Richmond Av., D.L.	T16 60
Richmond Cotts., Inchicore 8	F 9 41
Richmond Cres. 1	L 7 36
Richmond Ct. 6	L14 56
Richmond Estate 3	M 6 36
Richmond Gro., D.L.	T16 60
Richmond Hill 6	K11 49
Richmond Hill, D.L.	T16 60
Richmond Par. 1	L 7 36
Richmond Pl. 1	L 7 36
Richmond Pl., Rathmines 6	K11 49
Richmond Rd. 3	L 5 36
Richmond Row 6	K11 49
Richmond Row S. 2	K10 43
Richmond St. S.	
Richmond St. N. 1	L 7 36
Richmond St. S. 2	K10 43
Richmonds Cotts. 1	L 7 36
Richview Masonic School 14	M13 50
Richview Pk. 6	L13 50
Riddles Row 8	K 8 43
Ring St. 8	D10 40
Ring Ter. 8	E10 41
Ringsend Bridge	N 9 45
Ringsend Pk. 4	N 9 45
Ringsend Rd. 4	M 9 44
Rise, The, Drumcondra 9	K 4 23
Rise, The, Mount Merrion	P15 58
River Tolka Promenade 3	N 7 37
Riversdale Av. 6	J14 55
Riversdale Gro. 6	G13 48
Riverside Cotts. 6	G15 54
Riverside Dr. 14	J15 55
Road No. 1	O 8 45
Alexandra Rd.	
Road No. 21	O 8 45
Alexandra Rd.	
Road No. 31	O 8 45
Alexandra Rd.	
Robert Emmet Bridge	J11 49
Robert Pl. 3	L 6 36
Clonliffe Rd.	
Robert St. 3	L 6 36
Clonliffe Rd.	
Robert St. 8	H 9 42
Rock Hill, D.L.	R15 59
Rock Rd., D.L. (Inset)	P13 63
Rockfield Av. 12	E14 53
Rockfield Dr. 12	F13 47
Rockford Pk., D.L.	S16 59
Rockville Cres., D.L.	S16 59
Rockville Dr., D.L.	S16 59
Rockville Pk., D.L.	S16 59
Rockville Rd., D.L.	S16 59
Roebuck Av., Stillorgan	P15 58
Roebuck Castle 14	O15 57
Roebuck Downs 4	M15 56
Roebuck Rd. 14	M14 56
Rogers La. 2	L10 44
Rogersons Quay	M 8 44
Roncalli Rd., Kilbarrack	U 3 28
Roosevelt Cotts. 7	F 6 33
Rope Walk Pl. 4	N 9 45
Rory O'Connor Pk., D.L.	T17 60
Rory O'More Bridge	H 8 42
Rosary Gdns. E., D.L.	U16 60
Rosary Gdns. W., D.L.	U16 60
Rosary Rd. 8	H10 42
Rosary Ter. 4	N 9 45
Rosary Ter. E., D.L.	U16 60
Rosary Ter. W., D.L.	U16 60
Rosbeg Ct., Kilbarrack	U 3 28
Rose Glen Av. 5	T 3 28

Name	Grid
Rose Glen Rd. 5	S 3 27
Rose Pk., D.L.	T17 60
Rosemount 14	M14 56
Rosemount 14	M15 56
Rosemount Av. 5	P 4 26
Rosemount Pk. 14	M15 56
Rosemount Rd. 7	J 7 35
Rosemount Ter.	P14 58
Rosevale Ct. 5	Q 4 26
Rosmeen Gdns., D.L.	V16 61
Rosmeen Pk., D.L.	V17 61
Ross Rd. 8	J 9 43
Ross St. 7	H 7 34
Rossmore Av. 12	E15 53
Rossmore Clo. 12	E15 53
Rossmore Cres. 12	E15 53
Rossmore Dr. 12	E15 53
Rossmore Gro. 12	E15 53
Rossmore Lawn 12	E15 53
Rossmore Pk. 12	E16 53
Rossmore Rd. 12	E15 53
Rostrevor Rd. 6	J14 55
Rostrevor Ter. 6	J14 55
Rotunda Hospital 1	K 8 43
Rowan Park Av., Stillorgan	S16 59
Royal Canal Bank 7	J 7 35
Royal Canal Ter. 7	J 7 35
Royal City of Dublin Hospital 4	M10 44
Royal Hospital for Incurables 4	L11 50
Royal Marine Rd., D.L.	V16 61
Royal Ter. 3	M 6 36
Inverness Rd.	
Royal Ter. E., D.L.	V17 61
Royal Ter. N., D.L.	V17 61
Royal Ter. W., D.L.	V17 61
Royal Veterinary College 4	N10 45
Royal Victoria Eye & Ear Hospital 2	L10 44
Royse Rd. 7	J 6 35
Rugby Rd. 6	K11 49
Rugby Vill. 6	K11 49
Rugby Rd.	
Rushbrook Av. 12	D15 52
Rushbrook Ct., Tallaght	E15 53
Rushbrook Dr. 12	E15 53
Rushbrook Gro., Tallaght	E15 53
Rushbrook Pk., Tallaght	E15 53
Rushbrook Vw. 12	D15 52
Rushbrook Way, Tallaght	E15 53
Russell Av. 3	L 6 36
Russell Av. E. 3	M 8 44
Russell St. 1	L 7 36
Russell St. Bridge	L 7 36
Rutland Av. 12	H11 48
Rutland Gro. 12	H11 48
Rutland Pl. 3	P 6 38
Clontarf	
Rutland Pl. N. 1	L 7 36
Rutland Pl. W. 1	K 7 35
Rutland St. Lwr. 1	L 7 36
Rutland St. Upr. 1	L 7 36
Rutledges Ter. 8	H10 42
Ryders Row 1	K 8 43
Parnell St.	
Sackville Av. 3	L 7 36
Sackville Gdns. 3	L 7 36
Sackville La. 1	K 8 43
O'Connell St. Lwr.	
Sackville Pl. 1	K 8 43
St. Agnes Pk. 12	F12 47
St. Agnes Rd. 12	F13 47
St. Aidans Dr. 14	N15 57
St. Aidans Park Av. 3	N 6 37
St. Aidans Park Rd. 3	N 6 37
St. Aidans Pk. 3	N 6 37
St. Albans Pk. 4	P12 63
St. Albans Rd. 8	J10 43
St. Alphonsus Av. 9	K 6 35
St. Alphonsus Rd. 9	K 6 35
St. Andoens Ter. 8	J 9 43
Cook St.	
St. Andrews La. 2	K 9 43
Trinity St.	
St. Andrews St. 2	K 9 43
St. Annes 8	G13 48
St. Annes Av. 5	R 4 27
St. Annes City Hospital 6	L11 50
St. Annes Dr. 5	R 4 27
St. Annes Rd. N. 9	K 6 35
St. Annes Sq., D.L.	R15 59
St. Annes Ter. 5	R 4 27
St. Anthonys Cres. 12	D13 46
St. Anthonys Pl. 1	K 7 35
St. Anthonys Rd. 8	G10 42
St. Aongus Cres., Tallaght	C15 52
St. Aongus Gro., Tallaght	C15 52
St. Aongus Lawn, Tallaght	C15 52
St. Aongus Rd., Tallaght	C15 52
St. Assams Av. 5	S 4 27
St. Assams Dr. 5	S 4 27
St. Assams Pk. 5	S 4 27
St. Assams Rd. E. 5	S 4 27
St. Assams Rd. W. 5	S 4 27
St. Attracta Rd. 7	H 6 34
St. Audoens Ter. 8	J 9 43
School House La. W.	
St. Augustine St. 8	J 9 43
St. Barnabas Gdns. 3	M 7 36
St. Brendans Av. 5	P 3 26
St. Brendans Cotts. 4	N 9 45
St. Brendans Cres. 12	D14 52
St. Brendans Dr. 5	P 3 26
St. Brendans Hospital 7	H 7 34
St. Brendans Pk. 5	Q 3 26
St. Brendans Ter. 5	P 2 26
St. Brendans Ter., D.L.	U16 60
Library Rd.	
St. Bricins Hospital 7	H 8 42
St. Bricins Pk. 7	H 8 42
St. Bridgets Av. 12	D13 46
St. Bridgets Av. 3	M 7 36
St. Brigids Cres. 5	P 4 26
St. Brigids Dr. 5	P 4 26
St. Brigids Rd. Lwr. 9	K 6 35
St. Brigids Rd. Upr. 9	K 6 35
St. Brocs Cotts. 4	M12 50
St. Canices Pk. 11	J 3 23
St. Canices Rd. 11	J 3 23
St. Catherines Av. 8	H10 42
St. Catherines La. W. 8	J 9 43
St. Catherines Pk., D.L.	V17 61
St. Clares Av. 6	J11 49
Kimmage Rd. Lwr.	
St. Clares Hospital 9	J 4 23
St. Clares Ter. 6	J11 49
Mount Drummond Av.	
St. Clements 9	K 6 35
St. Clements Rd. 9	K 6 35
St. Columbas Rd. Lwr.	
St. Columbanus Av. 14	L14 56
St. Columbanus Pl. 14	L14 56
St. Columbanus Rd. 14	L14 56
St. Columbas Rd. 12	D13 46
St. Columbas Rd. Lwr. 9	K 6 35
St. Columbas Rd. Upr. 9	K 6 35
St. Conleths Rd. 12	D13 46
St. Davids Ter. 2	G 7 34
Blackhorse Av.	
St. Davids Ter. 9	K 4 23
Ballymun Rd.	
St. Davids Ter., Glasnevin 9	K 4 23
St. Declan Rd. 3	M 5 36
St. Declan Ter. 3	N 5 37
St. Donaghs Cres. 5	S 2 27
St. Donaghs Pk. 5	T 2 28
St. Donaghs Rd. 5	S 2 27
St. Eithne Rd. 7	H 6 34
St. Endas Dr. 14	H16 54
St. Endas Rd. 6	J13 49
St. Finbars Clo. 12	D14 52
St. Finbars Rd. 7	G 5 34
St. Fintan Rd. 7	H 6 34
St. Fintan Ter. 7	H 6 34
St. Fintans Cres., Howth	Y 4 30
St. Fintans Gro., Howth	Y 4 30
St. Fintans Pk., Howth	Y 4 30
St. Fintans Rd., Howth	Y 4 30
St. Gabriels Rd. 3	R 6 39
St. Gall Gdns. N. 14	L14 56
St. Gall Gdns. S. 14	L14 56
St. Georges Av. 3	L 6 36
St. Gerards Rd. 12	E13 47
St. Helena Rd. 11	F 4 21
St. Helenas Dr. 11	G 4 22
St. Helens Rd., D.L.	P14 58
St. Ignatius Av. 7	K 6 35
St. Ignatius Rd. 7	K 6 35
St. Itas Rd. 9	K 5 35
St. Jamess Av. 3	L 6 36
St. Jamess Av. 8	H 9 42
St. Jamess Pl. 8	E10 41
Tyrconnell Rd.	
St. Jamess Rd. 12	D13 46
St. Jamess Ter. 8	H10 42
St. Jarlath Rd. 7	H 6 34
St. Johns Av. 8	J 9 43
John St.	
St. Johns Ct. 3	O 5 37
St. Johns Pk., D.L.	U16 60
St. Johns Rd. E. 4	O11 51
St. Johns Rd., Kingsbridge 8	F 9 41
St. Johns St. 8	J10 43
Black Pitts	
St. Josephs Asylum 9	M 5 36
St. Josephs Av. 3	L 6 36
St. Josephs Av. 9	K 6 35
St. Josephs Childrens Hospital 1	K 7 35
St. Josephs College, D.L.	R15 59
St. Josephs Convent 6	H13 48
St. Josephs Par. 7	K 7 35
St. Josephs Pl. 7	H 7 34
Prussia St.	
St. Josephs Pl. 7	K 7 35
Dorset St. Upr.	
St. Josephs Rd. 12	D13 46
St. Josephs Rd. 7	H 7 34
St. Josephs Sq. 3	Q 7 38
Vernon Av.	
St. Josephs St. 7	K 7 35
Synnott Pl.	
St. Josephs Ter. 3	M 6 36
St. Kevins Gdns. 6	K13 49
St. Kevins Hospital 8	G 9 42
St. Kevins Par. 8	J10 43
St. Kevins Pk., Rathgar 6	K13 49
St. Kevins Rd. 8	J11 49
St. Kevins Vill., D.L.	U17 60
St. Killians Av. 12	D14 52
St. Laurence Gro. 10	C 9 40
St. Laurence Pk., Stillorgan	P16 58
St. Laurence Rd., Chapelizod	C 9 40
St. Laurence St. N. 1	M 8 44
Sheriff St. Lwr.	
St. Lawrence Hospitals 7	J 8 43
St. Lawrence Pl.	L 8 44
Sheriff St. Lwr.	
St. Lawrence Rd., Clontarf 3	O 6 37
St. Lawrence Rd., Howth	AA3 31
St. Lawrence St. 1	L 8 44
Sheriff St. Lwr.	
St. Lawrence Ter., Howth	BB3 31
St. Lukes Cres. 14	L14 56
St. Lukes Hospital 6	K14 55
St. Magdalene Ter. 4	N 9 45
St. Malachys Rd. 9	K 5 35
St. Malacys Dr. 12	D13 46
St. Margarets Av. 5	U 3 28
St. Margarets Av. N. 1	L 7 36
St. Margarets Ter. 8	H10 42
St. Martins Dr. 12	G13 48
St. Martins Pk. 12	H12 48
St. Marys Asylum 9	M 4 24
St. Marys Av. 4, Rathfarnham	H15 54
St. Marys Av. N. 7	K 7 35
St. Marys Av. W. 10	E 9 41
St. Marys Chest Hospital, Chapelizod	D 8 40
St. Marys College 4	M11 50
St. Marys College 6	K11 49
St. Marys College 9	M 5 36
St. Marys Cres. 12	E12 47
St. Marys Dr. 12	E11 47
St. Marys Home for Blind 4	P13 63
St. Marys Hospital 11	AA2 31
St. Marys La. 4	M10 44
St. Marys Pk. 12	E12 47
St. Marys Pl. 7	K 7 35
St. Marys Pl., Howth	BB3 31
Main St.	
St. Marys Rd. 12	E12 47
St. Marys Rd. N. 3	M 7 36
St. Marys Rd. S. 4	M10 44
St. Marys Rd., Howth (Inset)	BB2 31
Main St.	
St. Marys St., D.L.	U16 60
St. Marys Ter. 7	K 7 35
St. Mels Av. 12	D14 52
St. Michaels Hill 8	J 9 43
St. Michaels Hospital, D.L.	V16 61
St. Michaels La. 8	J 9 43
High St.	
St. Michaels Rd. 9	K 5 35
St. Michaels Ter. 8	J10 43
St. Michans St. 7	J 8 43
St. Mobhi Av. 9	K 4 23
St. Mobhi Boithirin 9	K 4 23
St. Mobhi Dr. 9	K 5 35
St. Mobhi Gro. 9	K 5 35
St. Mobhi Rd. 9	K 5 35
St. Mobhis Bridge	K 5 35
St. Nessans Ter., Howth	BB3 31
St. Nicholas Pl. 8	J 9 43
St. Pappin Grn 11	J 3 23
St. Pappin Rd. 11	J 3 23
St. Patrick Av. 3	M 7 36
North Strand Rd.	
St. Patricks Cathedral 8	J 9 43
St. Patricks Cotts. 14	H16 54
St. Patricks Cres., D.L.	T17 60
St. Patricks Home 7	E 5 33
St. Patricks Hospital 8	G 9 42
St. Patricks Parade 7	K 6 35
St. Patricks Rd., Walkinstown 12	D13 46
St. Patricks Rd., Drumcondra 9	K 6 35
St. Patricks Ter. 1	L 7 36
Russell St.	
St. Patricks Ter. 3	M 7 36
North Strand Rd.	
St. Patricks Ter. 8	E 9 41
St. Patricks Ter., D.L.	V17 61
Oliver Plunkett Rd.	
St. Patricks Training College 9	L 5 36
St. Patricks Vill. 4	N 9 45

Name	Ref
St. Paul St. 7	J 8 43
St. Pauls Ter., D.L.	W17 61
St. Peters Cres. 12	E13 47
St. Peters Dr. 12	E13 47
St. Peters Rd., Walkinstown 12	D13 46
St. Peters Rd., Phibsborough 7	J 6 35
St. Peters Ter., D.L.	W17 61
St. Peters Ter., Howth	AA3 31
St. Philomenas Rd. 11	J 6 35
St. Stephens Green Pk. 2	K10 43
St. Stephens Grn. E. 2	L10 44
St. Stephens Grn. N. 2	K 9 43
St. Stephens Grn. S. 2	K10 43
St. Stephens Grn. W. 2	K10 43
St. Teresas Monastery 6	H13 48
St. Teresas Pl. 9	J 5 35
Botanic. Av.	
St. Teresas Rd. 9	J 5 35
St. Teresas Rd., Crumlin 12	F13 47
St. Theresa Gdns. 8	H10 42
St. Thomas Rd., Tender Fields 4	J10 43
St. Thomas Rd., Stillorgan	O15 57
St. Thomass Av. 7	J 8 43
Constitution Hill	
St. Thomass Mead, Stillorgan	P15 58
St. Vincent St. N. 7	J 7 35
St. Vincent St. W. 8	E 9 41
St. Vincent St.,	J10 43
Tenter Fields 8	
St. Vincents Asylum 3	L 6 36
St. Vincents Home 7	E 5 33
St. Vincents Hospital 2	L10 44
St. Vincents Pk., D.L.	S15 59
Saints Dr. 5	R 4 27
(Raon Na Naomh)	
Salamanca 14	N15 57
Sallymount Av. 6	L11 50
Sallymount Gdns. 6	L11 50
Salzburg 14	N15 57
Sampsons La. 1	K 8 43
Sandford Av. 8	H10 42
Sandford Av., Donnybrook 4	M12 50
Sandford Gdns. 2	J10 43
Donore Av.	
Sandford Rd. 6	L12 50
Sandwith Pl. 2	L 9 44
Sandwith St. Lwr. 2	L 9 44
Sandwith St. Upr. 2	L 9 44
Sandycove Av. W., D.L.	W16 61
Sandycove Av. W., D.L.	W17 61
Sandycove Point, D.L.	W16 61
Sandycove Rd., D.L.	W17 61
Sandycove Station	V17 61
Sandyhill Av. 11	J 2 23
Sandymount Av. 4	N11 51
Sandymount Castle Dr. 4	O11 51
Sandymount Castle Rd. 4	O11 51
Sandymount Grn. 4	O10 45
Sandymount Rd. 4	P14 58
Sans Souci Pk., D.L.	P14 58
Sarsfield Quay 7	H 8 42
Sarsfield Rd. 10	D 9 40
Sarsfield St. 7	J 7 35
Sarto Rd., Kilbarrack	U 3 28
Saul Rd. 12	G11 48
School Av. 5	P 4 26
School House La. W. 8	J 9 43
School St. 8	H 9 42
Schoolhouse La. 2	L 9 44
Sea View Ter. 4	N12 51
Seabury 4	P12 63
Seacliff Av., Baldoyle	V 2 29
Seacliff Dr., Baldoyle	U 2 28
Seacourt 4	R 6 39
Seafield Av. 3	Q 6 38
Seafield Av., D.L.	T16 60
Seafield Clo., Stillorgan	O14 57
Seafield Cres., Stillorgan	P14 58
Seafield Dr., Booterstown	P14 58
Seafield Pk., Booterstown	P14 58
Seafield Rd. 4	O14 57
Seafield Rd. E. 3	Q 6 38
Seafield Rd. W. 3	P 6 38
Seafort Av. 4	O10 45
Seafort Cotts. 4	O10 45
Seafort Av.	
Seafort Gdns. 4	O10 45
Seafort Vill. 4	O10 45
Seagrange Av., Baldoyle	U 2 28
Seagrange Dr., Baldoyle	V 2 29
Seagrange Rd., Baldoyle	U 2 28
Sean Heuston Bridge	H 8 42
Sean McDermott St. Lwr. 1	L 7 36
Sean McDermott St. Upr. 1	K 8 43
Seapark Dr. 3	Q 6 38
Seapark Rd. 3	Q 6 38
Seapoint Av., D.L.	S15 59
Seaview Av. 3	M 7 36
Seaview Av. E. 1	M 7 36
Seaview Av. N. 3	O 6 37
Seaview Ter., Howth	BB3 31
Second Av. 1	M 8 44
Second Av., Rialto 8	G10 42
Serpentine Av. 4	N11 51
Serpentine Pk. 4	N10 45
Serpentine Rd. 4	N10 45
Serpentine Ter. 4	N11 51
Seven Oaks 9	L 4 24
Seventh Av. 8	G10 42
Seville Pl. 1	M 8 44
Seville Ter. 1	M 7 36
Shamrock Cotts. 1	M 7 36
Shamrock Pl.	
Shamrock Pl. 1	M 7 36
Shamrock St. 7	J 7 35
Primrose St.	
Shamrock Ter. 1	M 7 36
Shamrock Vill., Harolds Cross 6	H 1 48
Shamrock Villa 6	J12 49
Shanard Av. 9	K 3 23
Shanard Rd. 9	L 2 24
Shanboley Rd. 9	M 2 24
Shandon Cres. 7	J 6 35
Shandon Dr. 7	J 6 35
Shandon Gdns. 7	H 6 34
Shandon Pk. 7	J 6 35
Shandon Pk., D.L.	S15 59
Shandon Rd. 7	J 6 35
Shangan Av. 9	L 2 24
Shangan Gdns. 9	L 2 24
Shangan Grn. 9	L 2 24
Shangan Pk. 9	L 2 24
Shangan Rd. 9	K 2 23
Shangangh Rd. 9	K 6 35
Shanglas Rd. 9	M 3 24
Shanid Rd. 6	H13 48
Shanliss Av. 9	L 2 24
Shanliss Dr. 9	L 2 24
Shanliss Gro. 9	L 2 24
Shanliss Pk. 9	L 2 24
Shanliss Rd. 9	L 2 24
Shanliss Way 9	L 2 24
Shanliss Wk. 9	L 2 24
Shannon Ter. 8	G 9 42
Shanowen Av. 9	L 3 24
Shanowen Cres. 9	L 2 24
Shanowen Dr. 9	L 3 24
Shanowen Gro. 9	K 2 23
Shanowen Pk. 9	K 3 23
Shanowen Rd. 9	L 3 24
Shanrath Rd. 9	M 3 24
Shantalla Av. 9	M 3 24
Shantalla Dr. 9	M 3 24
Shantalla Pk. 9	M 3 24
Shantalla Rd. 9	M 3 24
Shanvarna Rd. 9	M 3 24
Shaw St. 2	L 9 44
Shaws La. 4	N10 45
Shelbourne Av. 4	N11 51
Shelbourne Rd.	
Shelbourne La. 4	N11 51
Shelbourne Park Greyhound Race Course 4	N 9 45
Shelbourne Rd. 4	N10 45
Shelmalier Rd. 3	M 7 36
Shelmartin Av. 3	M 6 36
Shelmartin Ter. 3	M 6 36
Shelton Dr. 12	F13 47
Shelton Gdns. 12	F13 47
Shelton Gro. 12	F13 47
Shelton Pk. 12	F13 47
Sheriff St. Lwr. 1	L 0 44
Sheriff St. Upr. 1	M 8 44
Sherkin Gdns. 9	L 4 24
Sherrard Av. 1	K 7 35
Sherrard St. Lwr. 1	K 7 35
Sherrard St. Upr. 1	K 7 35
Shielmartin Dr., Howth	Y 4 30
Shielmartin Pk., Howth	Y 4 30
Shielmartin Rd., Howth	Y 4 30
Ship St. Gt. 8	K 9 43
Ship St. Lit. 8	K 9 43
Shrewsbury Pk. 4	O11 51
Shrewsbury Rd. 4	N12 51
Sigurd Rd. 7	H 8 42
Silchester Cres., D.L.	V17 61
Silchester Pk., D.L.	V17 61
Silchester Rd., D.L.	V17 61
Silloge Av. 11	J 2 23
Silloge Gdns. 11	K 2 23
Silloge Rd. 11	J 2 23
Silver Birches 14	M16 56
Silverwood Dr. 14	G16 54
Silverwood Dr. 14	F15 53
Templeville Dr.	
Silverwood Rd. 14	G16 54
Simonscourt Castle 4	N12 51
Simonscourt Rd. 4	N11 51
Simonscourt, Donnybrook 4	M12 50
Sion Hill Av. 9	H12 48
Sion Hill Rd. 9	M 4 24
Sir John Rogersons Quay 2	M 8 44
Sir Patrick Duns Hospital 2	M 9 44
Sitric Rd. 7	H 8 42
Sixth Av. 8	G10 42
Skellys La. 5	N 3 25
Skippers Alley 8	J 9 43
Skreen Rd 7	F 6 33
Slademore Clo. 5	R 2 27
Slademore Dr. 5	R 2 27
Slane Rd. 12	G11 48
Slaney Rd. 11	H 5 34
Slemish Rd. 7	F 6 33
Slieve Rua Dr., Stillorgan	O16 57
Slievebloom Pk. 12	E11 47
Slievebloom Rd. 12	E11 47
Slievemore Rd. 12	F11 47
Slievenamon Rd. 12	G10 42
Sloperton, D.L.	U16 60
Smithfield 7	J 8 43
Smiths Vill., D.L.	U16 60
Somerset St. 4	N 9 45
Somerville Av. 12	E12 47
Somerville Pk. 12	E12 47
Sorbonne 14	N15 57
South Av., Stillorgan	P16 58
South Circular Rd. 8	E 8 41
South Great Georges St. 2	K 9 43
South Hill 6	L13 50
South Hill Av., D.L.	P15 58
South Hill Pk., D.L.	P15 58
South Lotts Rd. 4	N10 45
South Rd. No. 4 1	P 8 62
Alexandra Rd.	
Southern Cross Av. 8	F 9 41
Southwood Pk., D.L.	Q15 58
Spa Rd. 8	E 9 41
Spafield Ter. 4	N11 51
Spencer Av. 1	M 8 44
Spencer Dock 1	M 8 44
Guild St.	
Spencer St. 8	J10 43
South Circular Rd.	
Spencer St. N. 3	M 7 36
Spencer Vill., D.L.	W17 61
Sperrin Rd. 12	E11 47
Spire View La. 6	J12 49
Spitalfields 8	J 9 43
Spring Garden St. 3	M 7 36
Springdale Rd. 5	Q 3 26
Springfield 7	F 6 33
Springfield Av. 6	G15 54
Springfield Cres. 6	G15 54
Springfield Dr. 6	G15 54
Springfield Pk. 6	G15 54
Springfield Rd. 6	G15 54
Square, The, 4	N 9 45
Square, The, 6	H12 48
Stable La. 4	N10 45
Stamer St. 8	K10 43
Stanaway.Dr. 12	G12 48
Stanford Grn. 12	E12 47
Stannaway Av. 12	F12 47
Stannaway Rd. 12	G12 48
Station Rd. 5	R 4 27
Station Rd., D.L.	W17 61
Station Rd., Sutton	W 2 29
Steevens Hospital 8	H 9 42
Steevens La. 8	H 9 42
Stella Av. 9	K 4 23
Stephen St. Upr. 8	K 9 43
Stephens La. 2	M10 44
Stephens Pl. 2	L10 44
Stephens Rd. 8	F10 41
Stiles Rd., The, 3	O 6 37
Stillorgan Park Av., Stillorgan	Q16 58
Stillorgan Pk., Stillorgan	Q16 58
Stillorgan Rd., Stillorgan 4	N12 51
Stirrup La. 7	J 8 43
Beresford St.	
Stoneview Pl., D.L.	V16 61
Stoney Rd. 3	M 7 36
East Wall Rd.	
Stoney Rd., Dundrum 14	M16 56
Stoneybatter 7	H 8 42
Store St. 1	L 8 44
Stormanstown Rd. 11	J 3 23
Stradbrook Gdns., D.L.	S16 59
Stradbrook Rd.	
Stradbrook Hall, D.L.	S16 59
Stradbrook Lawn, D.L.	S16 59
Stradbrook Pk., D.L.	S16 59
Stradbrook Rd., D.L.	S16 59
Stradbrook, D.L.	S16 59
Strand Rd., Howth	Y 4 30
Strand Rd., Sandymount 4	O11 51
Strand St. 4	N 9 45
Strand St. Gt. 1	K 8 43
Strand St. Lit. 7	K 8 43
Strandville Av. E. 3	O 6 37
Strandville Av. N. 3	M 7 36
Strandville House 3	O 6 37
Strangford Gdns. 3	M 7 36
Strangford Rd. 3	M 7 36
Stratford Row 1	L 7 36
Streamville Rd. 5	S 2 27

Name	Grid
Suffolk St. 2	K 9 43
Suir Rd. 8	F10 41
Sullivan St. 7	G 8 42
Summer St. N. 1	L 7 36
Summer St. S. 8	H 9 42
Summerhill 1	L 7 36
Summerhill Par. 1	L 7 36
Summerhill Pl. 1	L 7 36
Summerhill Rd., D.L.	V16 61
Summerville 14	M15 56
Summerville Pk. 6	K12 49
Sunbury Gdns. 6	K13 49
Sundrive Pk. 12	H12 48
Sundrive Rd. 12	G11 48
Susan Ter. 8	J10 43
Susanville Rd. 3	L 6 36
Sussex St., D.L.	L11 50
Sussex St., D.L.	V16 61
Sussex Ter. Lwr. 4	L10 44
Mespil Rd.	
Sussex Ter. Upr. 4	L11 50
Leeson St. Upr.	
Sutton Boulevard S., Kilbarrack	U 3 28
Sutton Ct., Kilbarrack	V 3 29
Sutton Downs, Kilbarrack	V 3 29
Sutton Gro., Kilbarrack	V 2 29
Swan Pl. 4	M11 50
Morehampton Rd.	
Swan Yd. 2	K 9 43
Harry St.	
Swans Nest Av. 5	T 3 28
Swans Nest Ct. 5	T 3 28
Swans Nest Rd. 5	S 2 27
Sweetmans Av., D.L.	R15 59
Sweetmount Av. 14	L16 56
Sweetmount Dr. 14	L16 56
Sweetmount Pk. 14	L16 56
Swifts Alley 8	J 9 43
Swifts Row 1	J 9 43
Ormond Quay Upr.	
Swilly Rd. 7	G 6 34
Swords Rd. 9	L 2 24
Swords Rd. N. 9	L 4 24
Swords St. 7	H 8 42
Sybil Hill Av. 5	Q 4 26
Sybil Hill Rd. 5	Q 4 26
Sycamore Cres., Stillorgan	P15 58
Sycamore Pk. 11	H 2 22
Sycamore Rd., Finglas 11	H 2 22
Sycamore Rd., Mt. Merrion	P15 58
Sycamore St. 2	K 9 43
Sydenham Rd., Dundrum 14	M16 56
Sydenham Rd., Sandymount 4	N11 51
Sydenham Vill. 14	M16 56
Sydney Av., D.L.	R15 59
Sydney Parade Av. 4	O12 51
Sydney Ter., D.L.	R15 59
Synge St. 8	K10 43
Synnott Pl. 7	K 7 35
Synnott Row 7	K 7 35
Talbot La. 1	L 8 44
Talbot St.	
Talbot Pl. 1	L 8 44
Talbot St. 1	L 8 44
Tallaght Rd., Tallaght	C16 52
Taney Av. 14	M16 56
Taney Cres. 14	M16 56
Taney Dr. 14	M16 56
Taney Gro. 14	N16 57
Taney Lawn 14	M16 56
Taney Manor 14	M16 56
Taney Pk. 14	M16 56
Taney Rd. 14	M16 56
Taney Rise 14	M16 56
Tara Hill Cres. 14	H16 54
Tara Hill Gro. 14	H16 54
Tara Hill Rd. 14	H16 54
Tara Lawn 5	S 2 27
Tara St. 2	L 8 44
Tara Street Station	L 8 44
Taylors La. 8	H 9 42
Teach Ultain 2	K11 49
Temple Bar 2	K 9 43
Temple Cotts. 7	J 7 35
Temple Cres., D.L.	S15 59
Temple Gdns. 6	K13 49
Temple Hill, D.L.	S15 59
Temple La. N. 1	K 7 35
Temple La. S. 2	K 9 43
Temple Park Av., D.L.	S15 59
Temple Pk. 6	L13 50
Temple Rd. 6	K13 49
Temple Rd., D.L.	R15 59
Temple St. N. 1	K 7 35
Temple St. W. 7	H 8 42
Temple Vill. 6	K12 49
Palmerston Rd.	
Templemore Av. 6	K13 49
Templeogue Wood Heights 12	F15 53
Templeogue Wood 12	F15 53
Templeville Av. 6	F15 53

Name	Grid
Templeville Dr. 6	F15 53
Templeville Pk. 6	G15 54
Templeville Rd. 6	F14 53
Terenure College 6	G14 54
Terenure Pk. 6	H13 48
Terenure Pl. 6	H13 48
Terenure Rd. E. 6	H13 48
Terenure Rd. N. 6	H13 48
Terenure Rd. W. 6	G13 48
Terminal Rd. N. 1	P 8 62
Terminal Rd. S. 1	P 8 62
Thatch Rd., The, 9	M 4 24
Third Av. 1	M 8 44
Third Av. 8	H10 42
Dolphins Barn	
Third Av., Rialto 8	G10 42
Thomas Ct. 8	J 9 43
Thomas Davis St. S. 8	J 9 43
Thomas Davis St. W. 8	E10 41
Thomas La. 1	K 8 43
Thomas Moore Rd. 12	D12 46
Thomas St. E. 4	N 9 45
Thomas St. W. 8	H 9 42
Thomond Rd. 10	C 9 40
Thor Pl. 7	H 8 42
Thormanby Lawns, Howth	BB3 31
Thormanby Rd., Howth	BB3 31
Thormanby Woods, Howth	BB4 31
Thorncastle St. 4	N 9 45
Thorncliffe Pk. 14	K14 55
Thorndale Av.	O 4 25
Elm Mount Rd.	
Thorndale Cres.	O 4 25
Elm Mount Rd.	
Thorndale Ct. 9	M 4 24
Thorndale Dr. 5	O 4 25
Thorndale Gro. 5	O 4 25
Thorndale Lawn	O 4 25
Elm Mount Rd.	
Thorndale Pk.	O 4 25
Elm Mount Rd.	
Thornhill Rd., Stillorgan	O16 57
Thornville Av. 5	T 3 28
Thornville Dr. 5	T 3 28
Thornville Pk., Kilbarrack	T 3 28
Thornville Rd. 5	T 3 28
Three Rock Clo. 12	C14 52
Kilmashogue Gro.	
Tibradden Clo. 12	C14 52
Tibradden Dr.	
Tibradden Dr. 12	C14 52
Tibradden Gro. 12	C14 52
Tibradden Dr.	
Timber Quay 1	O 8 45
Tivoli Clo., D.L.	U17 60
Tivoli Rd., D.L.	U16 60
Tivoli Ter. E., D.L.	U16 60
Tivoli Ter. N., D.L.	U16 60
Tivoli Ter. S., D.L.	U16 60
Tolka Cotts. 11	H 4 22
Tolka Estate Rd. 11	J 4 23
Tolka Quay 1	O 8 45
Tolka Quay Rd. 1	P 8 62
Tolka View Ter. 11	H 4 22
Tom Clarke House 3	M 6 36
Tom Kelly Rd. 2	K11 49
Tonduff Clo. 12	C14 52
Lugnaquilla Av.	
Tonguefield Rd. 12	G12 48
Tonlegee Av. 5	R 2 27
Tonlegee Dr. 5	Q 2 26
Tonlegee Rd. 5	Q 2 26
Torlogh Gdns. 3	M 6 36
Torlogh Par. 3	M 5 36
Tourmakeady Rd. 9	L 3 24
Tower Av. 6	J13 49
Tower View Cotts. 11	J 5 35
Townsend St. 2	L 9 44
Trafalgar La., D.L.	S15 59
Trafalgar Ter., D.L.	S15 59
Tram St. 3	Q 7 38
Tramway Cotts. 7	J 6 35
Tramway Ter. 4	O11 51
Tramway Vill. 6	H13 48
Tranquility Gro. 5	O 2 25
Trees Av., Stillorgan	P16 58
Trees Rd., Stillorgan	O16 57
Trevor Ter. 2	M 9 44
Greenore Ter.	
Trimleston Av., Booterstown	P13 63
Trimleston Dr., Stillorgan	P13 63
Trimleston Gdns., Stillorgan	P13 63
Trimleston Pk., Stillorgan	P13 63
Trimleston Rd., Stillorgan	P13 63
Trinity College 2	L 9 44
Trinity St. 2	K 9 43
Tritonville Av. 4	O10 45
Tritonville Cres. 4	O10 45
Tritonville Ct. 4	O10 45
Tritonville Rd. 4	N10 45
Tryconnell Pk. 8	E10 41

Name	Grid
Tucketts La., Howth	AA3 31
Tudor Rd. 6	L13 50
Tuscany Downs 5	R 3 27
Tuscany Park, Baldoyle	V 2 29
Tymon Castle, Tallaght	D15 52
Tymon La., Tallaght	C14 52
Tymon North Gdns., Tallaght	C15 52
Tymon North Grn., Tallaght	C15 52
Tymon North Lawn, Tallaght	C15 52
Tymon North Pk., Tallaght	C15 52
Tymon North Rd., Tallaght	C15 52
Tymonville Av., Tallaght	C15 52
Tymonville Cres., Tallaght	C15 52
Tymonville Ct., Tallaght	C15 52
Tymonville Dr., Tallaght	C15 52
Tymonville Gro., Tallaght	C15 52
Tymonville Pk., Tallaght	C15 52
Tymonville Rd., Tallaght	C15 52
Tyrconnell Rd. 8	E10 41
Tyrconnell St. 8	E10 41
Tyrconnell Vill. 8	E 9 41
Gratan Cres.	
Tyrone Pl. 8	E10 41
Tyrone Sq. 8	E10 41
U.S.A. Embassy 8	D 7 32
Ulster St. 7	J 6 35
Union Pl., Haroldscross 6	H11 48
University College 2	K10 43
Upper Cliff Rd., Howth	BB3 31
Uppercross Rd. 8	G10 42
Usher St. 8	J 9 43
Ushers Island 8	H 8 42
Ushers Quay 8	J 9 43
Valentia Par. 7	K 7 35
Valentia Rd. 9	L 4 24
Valeview Cres. 11	G 4 22
Valeview Dr. 11	F 4 21
Valeview Gdns. 11	F 4 21
Valley Park Av. 11	E 4 21
Valley Park Dr. 11	E 4 21
Valley Park Rd. 11	E 4 21
Vavasour Sq. 4	N10 45
Ventry Dr. 7	G 5 34
Ventry Pk. 7	G 5 34
Ventry Rd. 7	G 5 34
Verbena Av., Kilbarrack	U 3 28
Verbena Av., Kilbarrack	U 2 28
Verbena Pk., Kilbarrack	U 2 28
Vergemount 6	L13 50
Milltown	
Vergemount Hall 6	M12 50
Vergemount Isolation Hospital 6	M13 50
Vergemount Pk. 6	M12 50
Vernon Av. 6	K13 49
Frankfort Av.	
Vernon Av., Clontarf 3	P 5 38
Vernon Dr. 3	Q 5 38
Vernon Gdns. 3	Q 6 38
Vernon Gro. 3	Q 6 38
Vernon Gro., Rathgar 6	K13 49
Vernon Par. 3	O 6 37
Clontarf Rd.	
Vernon Pk. 3	Q 6 38
Vernon Rd. 3	Q 5 38
Vernon St. 8	J10 43
Vernon Ter. 6	K13 49
Frankfort Av.	
Veronica Ter. 4	N 9 45
Verschoyle Ct. 2	M 9 44
Mount St. Lwr.	
Verschoyle Pl. 2	L10 44
Stephens Pl.	
Vesey Pl., D.L.	U16 60
Vesey Ter., Rathgar 6	J13 49
Veterinary Laboratory 9	M 4 24
Vicar St. 8	J 9 43
Victoria Av. 4	M12 50
Victoria Quay 8	H 8 42
Victoria Rd., Clontarf 3	O 6 37
Victoria Rd., Terenure 6	J14 55
Victoria St. 8	J10 43
Victoria Ter. 14	M16 56
Victoria Ter. 3	Q 7 38
Clontarf Rd.	
Victoria Ter., D.L.	V16 61
Victoria Vill. 3	N 6 37
Malahide Rd.	
Victoria Vill., Rathgar 6	J13 49
Viking Pl. 7	H 8 42
Arbour Hill	
Viking Rd. 7	H 8 42
Villa Park Av. 7	F 6 33
Villa Park Dr. 7	F 6 33
(Ceide Phairc An Bhailtini)	
Villa Park Gdns. 7	F 6 33
(Gardini Phairc An Bhailtini)	
Villa Park Rd. 7	F 6 33
(Br. Phairc An Bhailtini)	
Village, The 5	S 4 27

Name	Ref
Villarea Pk., D.L.	W17 61
Villiers Rd. 6	K13 49
Vincent St. 8	J10 43
Vincent Ter. 9	K 5 35
Violet Hill Dr. 11	H 4 22
Violet Hill Pk. 11	H 4 22
Violet Hill Rd. 11	H 4 22
Virginia Dr. 11	F 3 21
Virginia Pk.	
Virginia Pk. 11	F 3 21
Wad Bridge	K 3 23
Wadelai Grn. 11	K 3 23
Wadelai Rd. 11	J 3 23
Wades Av. 5	R 4 27
Wainsfort Av. 6	F14 53
Wainsfort Cres. 6	F14 53
Wainsfort Dr. 6	F13 47
Wainsfort Gdns. 6	F14 53
Wainsfort Cres.	
Wainsfort Gro. 6	G14 54
Wainsfort Pk. 6	G14 54
Wainsfort Rd. 6	F14 53
Waldemar Ter. 14	L16 56
Waldrons Bridge	
Walkinstown Av. 12	D12 46
Walkinstown Cres. 12	D12 46
Walkinstown Dr. 12	D12 46
Walkinstown Grn. 12	D12 46
Walkinstown Par. 12	D12 46
Walkinstown Pk. 12	D12 46
Walkinstown Rd. 12	D12 46
Wallace Rd. 12	E12 47
Walnut Av. 9	L 4 24
Walnut Ct. 9	L 4 24
Walnut Lawn 9	L 4 24
Walnut Pk. 9	L 4 24
Walnut Rise 9	L 4 24
Walsh Rd. 9	K 5 35
Waltham Ter., D.L.	Q15 58
Walworth Rd. 8	J10 43
Victoria St.	
Wards Hill 8	J10 43
Warren St. 8	K11 49
Warrenhouse Rd., Baldoyle	W 2 29
Warrenmount 8	J10 43
Warrenmount Pl. 8	J10 43
Warrenpoint 3	O 6 37
Warrington La. 2	M10 44
Warrington Pl.	
Warrington Pl. 2	M10 44
Warwick Ter. 6	L11 50
Sallymount Av.	
Wasdale Gro. 6	J14 55
Wasdale Pk. 6	J14 55
Washington La. 14	G16 54
Washington Pk. 14	G15 54
Washington St. 8	J10 43
Waterfall Av. 3	L 6 36
Waterfall Rd. 5	R 4 27
Waterloo Av. 3	M 7 36
Waterloo La. 4	L11 50
Waterloo Rd. 4	M11 50
Watermill Av. 5	R 4 27
Watermill Bridge	S 5 39
Watermill Dr. 5	R 4 27
Watermill Pk. 5	R 4 27
Watermill Rd. 5	R 4 27
(Br. An Easa)	
Watling St. 8	H 9 42
Waverley Av. 3	M 6 36
Waverley Ter. 6	J12 49
Kenilworth Rd.	
Weavers La. 7	J 7 35
Phibsborough Rd.	
Weavers Sq. 8	J10 43
Wellesley Pl. 1	L 7 36
Russell St.	
Wellington Cotts. 12	E14 53
Wellington La. 12	E14 53
Wellington La. 4	M11 50
Wellington Monument	G 8 42
Wellington Pk. 12	E14 53
Wellington Pl. N. 7	K 7 35
Wellington Pl., Donnybrook 4	M11 50
Wellington Quay 2	K 9 43
Wellington St. 7	K 7 35
Wellington St., D.L.	U16 60
Wellmount Av. 11	F 3 21
Wellmount Cres. 11	F 3 21
Wellmount Ct. 11	F 3 21
Wellmount Dr. 11	F 3 21
Wellmount Grn. 11	F 3 21
Wellmount Pk. 11	F 3 21
Wellmount Rd. 11	F 3 21
Wellpark Av. 9	L 5 36
Wentworth Ter. 2	M 9 44
Hogan Pl.	
Werburgh St. 8	J 9 43
Wesley Pl. 8	J11 49
Wesley Rd. 6	J13 49
West Oil Jetty 1	P 9 62
West Park Dr.11	J 4 23
West Pk. 5	Q 3 26
West Rd. 3	M 7 36
West Ter. 8	E 9 41
Westbourne Rd. 6	H14 54
Westbrook Rd. 14	L15 56
Western Rd. 8	H10 42
Donore Av.	
Western Way 7	J 7 35
Westfield Rd. 6	H12 48
Westhampton Pl. 6	H13 48
Terenure Rd. N.	
Westland Row 2	L 9 44
Westmoreland Pk. 6	L11 50
Westmoreland St. 2	K 9 43
Weston Av. 14	L16 56
Weston Clo. 14	L16 56
Weston Gro. 14	L16 56
Weston Pk. 14	L16 56
Weston Rd. 14	L16 56
Westwood Av. 11	E 3 21
Westwood Rd. 11	E 3 21
Wexford St. 2	K10 43
Wharton Ter. 6	J11 49
Harolds Cross Rd.	
Whitebarn Rd. 14	K15 55
Whitebeam Av. 14	M13 50
Whitebeam Rd. 14	M13 50
Whitechurch Rd. 14	H16 54
Whitefriar Pl. 8	K 9 43
Aungier St.	
Whitefriar St. 8	K 9 43
Whitehall Gdns. 12	F13 47
Whitehall Pk. 12	E14 53
Whitehall Rd. E. 12	E14 53
Whitehall Rd. W. 12	E14 53
Whitehall Rd., Rathfarnham 14	K16 55
Whites La. N. 7	J 7 35
Whitethorn Av. 5	O 3 25
Whitethorn Clo. 5	N 4 25
Whitethorn Cres. 5	O 3 25
Whitethorn Gro. 5	O 3 25
Whitethorn La. 4	N 9 45
Thorncastle St.	
Whitethorn Pk. 5	O 3 25
Whitethorn Rd. 14	M13 50
Whitethorn Rd. 5	N 3 25
Whitethorn Ri. 5	O 4 25
Whitton Rd. 6	H13 48
Whitworth Av. 3	K 6 35
Whitworth Pl.	
Whitworth Pl. 3	K 6 35
Whitworth Rd. 1	M 8 44
Seville Pl.	
Whitworth Rd. 9	J 6 35
Whitworth Row 1	M 7 36
Wicklow La. 2	K 9 43
Wicklow St.	
Wicklow St. 2	K 9 43
Wigan Rd. 9	K 6 35
Wilfrid Rd. 6	J12 49
Willbrook Pk. 14	H16 54
Willbrook Rd. 14	H16 54
Willbrook St. 14	H16 54
Willfield Pk. 4	O11 51
Willfield Rd. 4	O11 51
William St. N. 1	L 7 36
William St. S. 2	K 9 43
Williams La. 1	K 8 43
Princes St. N.	
Williams Pk. 6	K11 49
Williams Pl. S. 8	J10 43
Williams Pl. Upr. 1	K 6 35
Williams Row 1	K 8 43
Willington Av. 12	E14 53
Willington Cres., Tallaght	E15 53
Willington Dr., Tallaght	E15 53
Willington Grn. 12	E14 53
Willington Gro. 12	E15 53
Willington Pk. 12	E15 53
Willington Gro.	
Willmont Av., D.L.	W17 61
Willow Bank, D.L.	U16 60
Willow Park Av. 11	J 2 23
Willow Park Clo. 11	J 2 23
Willow Park Cres. 11	H 2 22
Willow Park Dr. 11	J 2 23
Willow Park Gro. 11	J 2 23
Willow Park Lawn 11	J 2 23
Willow Park Rd. 11	J 2 23
Willow Pl., Booterstown	Q14 58
Willow Ter., D.L.	Q14 58
Rock Rd.	
Willowbank Pk. 14	G16 54
Windele Rd. 9	O11 51
Windmill Av. 12	F12 47
Windmill La. 2	M 9 44
Windmill Pk. 12	F12 47
Windmill Rd. 12	F11 47
Windsor Av. 3	M 6 36
Windsor Ct., D.L.	T17 60
Stradbrook Rd.	
Windsor Dr., D.L.	T17 60
Windsor Pk., D.L.	T17 60
Windsor Rd. 6	K12 49
Windsor Ter. 8	J11 49
Windsor Ter., D.L.	V16 61
Windsor Vill. 3	M 6 36
Winetavern St. 8	J 9 43
Winton Av. 6	J13 49
Winton Rd. 6	L11 50
Wolfe Tone Av., D.L.	U16 60
Wolfe Tone Quay 7	H 8 42
Wolfe Tone St. 1	K 8 43
Wolseley St. 8	J10 43
Wood Quay 8	J 9 43
Wood St. 8	K 9 43
Woodbank Av. 11	E 4 21
Woodbank Dr. 11	E 4 21
Woodbine Av., Stillorgan	O14 57
Woodbine Clo. 5	R 3 27
Woodbine Dr. 5	R 3 27
Woodbine Pk. 5	R 3 27
Woodbine Pk., Booterstown	P13 63
Woodbine Rd. 5	S 2 27
Woodbine Rd., Stillorgan 4	O13 51
Woodbrook Pk. 14	F16 53
Woodcliff Heights, Howth	BB3 31
Woodfield Av. 10	E 9 41
Woodfield Pl. 10	E 9 41
Woodfield Av.	
Woodland Pk., Stillorgan	P15 58
Woodland Vill. 2	L11 50
Woodlands Av., Stillorgan	P16 58
Woodlands Dr., Stillorgan	P16 58
Woodlawn Cres. 14	L15 56
Woodlawn Pk. 14	L15 56
Woodlawn Pk., D.L.	U17 60
Woodlawn Ter. 14	L16 56
Woodside 14	J15 55
Woodside Gro. 14	J15 55
Woodstock Gdns. 6	L12 50
Woodview Clo. 5	S 2 27
Woodview Cotts. 14	H15 54
Woodview Pk. 5	S 2 27
Woodville Rd. 9	K 5 35
Botanic Av.	
Wynberg Pk., D.L.	S16 59
Wynnefield Rd. 6	K12 49
Wynnsward Dr. 14	M14 56
Wynnsward Pk. 14	M14 56
Xavier Av. 3	M 7 36
Yankee Ter., Stillorgan	R16 59
Yellow Rd. 9	M 4 24
York Av. 6	K12 49
York Rd. 4	N 9 45
York Rd., D.L.	U16 60
York Rd., Rathmines 6	K12 49
York St. 2	K 9 43
York Ter., D.L.	U16 60
Zion Rd. 6	J14 55
Zoological Gdns. 8	F 7 33